LINCOLN CHRISTIAN COLLEGE AND SEMINARY

P9-CRQ-995

Addiction

Addiction

PASTORAL RESPONSES

Bucky Dann

EDITED BY DANIEL G. BAGBY

ABINGDON PRESS

NASHVILLE

ADDICTION
PASTORAL RESPONSES

Copyright © 2002 by Abingdon Press

All rights reserved.
No part of this work may be reproduced or transmitted in any form or by any means, electronic or mechanical, including photocopying and recording, or by any information storage or retrieval system, except as may be expressly permitted by the 1976 Copyright Act or in writing from the publisher. Requests for permission should be addressed to Abingdon Press, P.O. Box 801, 201 Eighth Avenue South, Nashville, TN 37202-0801.

This book is printed on elemental-chlorine–free paper.

Library of Congress Cataloging-in-Publication Data

Dann, Bucky, 1951-
    Addiction : pastoral responses / Bucky Dann ; edited by Daniel G. Bagby.
        p. cm.
    ISBN 0-687-04504-5 (pbk. :alk. paper)
    1. Church work with alcoholics. 2. Church work with narcotic addicts.
    3. Pastoral counseling. I. Bagby, Daniel G. II. Title.
    BV4460.5 .D36 2002
    261.8'32292—dc21

                                                                    2002008434

Scripture quotations marked NJB are from THE NEW JERUSALEM BIBLE, copyright © 1985 by Darton, Longman & Todd, Ltd. and Doubleday, a division of Random House, Inc. Reprinted by permission.

Scripture quotations marked TEV are from the Today's English Version—Second Edition. Copyright © 1992 by American Bible Society. Used by permission.

Scripture quotations marked NASB are from THE NEW AMERICAN STANDARD BIBLE®, Copyright © The Lockman Foundation 1960, 1962, 1963, 1968, 1971, 1972, 1973, 1975, 1977. Used by permission.

02 03 04 05 06 07 08 09 10 11—10 9 8 7 6 5 4 3 2 1

MANUFACTURED IN THE UNITED STATES OF AMERICA

To

Rita, Jennie, Kevin, and Alissa

in gratitude,

for welcoming me into their family,

with grace and love

114334

Contents

Introduction

Chances are your church is not immune to the drug demographics in America. It is estimated that nearly fourteen million adult Americans have alcohol-abuse problems.[1] Forty-three percent of American families report having an alcoholic member.[2] A recent study of fifty thousand teenagers found that, among eighth graders, 1.3 percent had tried heroin, 2.1 percent had smoked crack, 11.1 percent had used inhalants (glue, paint thinner, aerosols), and 22 percent had smoked marijuana.[3] Although not all of these teenagers will become addicted, drug abuse statistics indicate that religious communities should expect to have congregants of all ages who use drugs abusively or addictively. The question is, Do you recognize them? If you recognize their addictions, what should you do?

Looking back on my years in the ministry, I realize how little I knew or suspected about the drug use of my parishioners. Occasionally it was a problem that could not be missed, as with the man who was infamous in town for becoming violent when drunk. Often I was blind to a person's addiction until it was brought directly to my attention, which explains my surprise when an active parishioner confessed to me her long-term use of Valium and struggles with withdrawal. However, confessions like this were few, and I am sure I overlooked a great deal of drug and alcohol abuse.

Just as important as my ignorance about drug addiction

was my inability to offer effective ministry to those who did gain my attention or confess. When the parishioner who was addicted to Valium talked with me one day, I did not say much. Truthfully, I did not know what to say. When a villager walked in off the street and wanted help with his alcoholism, I called a parishioner who I knew was in Alcoholics Anonymous (AA). Although referral can be helpful, it was the limit of my expertise. Comparably, the only ministry extended to the addicted by the churches I led was giving free space for AA meetings.

For many congregations, this is the usual ministry. But it is a ministry that can be changed for the better. Twelve Step programs, overtly centered upon spirituality and connection with a higher power, have been the most effective means of recovery for alcoholics and drug addicts. All religious communities are positioned to offer life-giving spirituality similar to Twelve Step programs to a significant group of people, but doing so requires intention and understanding.

There are several ways in which the church is uniquely situated to help people who abuse alcohol and drugs. For example, the most successful remedy remains some sort of spiritual program. A study of treatment outcomes published in the *Journal of Alcohol Studies* (January 1997) reported that the Twelve Step method used by Alcoholics Anonymous and Narcotics Anonymous (NA) proved as effective as therapies that required professional counselors. Furthermore, people more often attend AA and NA meetings than participate in therapy. The church is already involved in a form of remediation sought by many addicts and has a built-in basis for communication, once the points of connection are understood. In addition, the church is able to offer a fuller form of spirituality. As profound as the Twelve Steps are, they are intended neither to speak to a wide variety of human dilemmas nor to provide sacred rites for the passages of life. The Christian community could learn a great deal from a study of the Steps but can go beyond them in helping people understand God, life, and our place in the world.

Another advantage of churches is that pastors and priests are uniquely positioned to recognize those who suffer from addiction. The symptoms of drug abuse are mostly contextual within the behaviors and relationships of a person's everyday life. More than any clinician, clergy are able to observe people in their own environments and often have intimate knowledge of personal circumstances. This knowledge makes clergy more likely to discern drug or drinking issues before they become severe enough to require treatment. This is especially true because clergy are frequently the first resort for guidance when one faces personal difficulties. During my years in church ministry, I saw myself as a medic, dispensing aid for all sorts of problems and attempting to get people into more intensive care, whether that was with a doctor or psychiatrist or social worker. If I had known more about drug abuse or addiction, I could undoubtedly have moved people into recovery or treatment.

Churches are also well situated to help addicts transition back into their communities. The attitudes within American culture toward addiction are deeply divided; whereas addicts are labeled as ill by the medical establishment, the cultural response is often punitive and judgmental. A biblical comparison can be made with the fear of lepers who were declared unclean and exiled from the community of "normals." Addicts and alcoholics are very aware of the shame attached to their condition and often resist sharing this aspect of their lives. Churches and clergy can bridge this gap of pain and mistrust, first, by educating themselves and, then, by educating others so that a truly open community is offered to this stigmatized group.

Without question, the social costs generated by active addicts are high. But punishment and ostracism do not change addicts and may make the situation worse. Churches are in a position to do more than offer their facilities as meeting places for AA, NA, and other associated gatherings. They can directly address the nature and presence of addiction. They can provide compassion, understanding, and fellowship.

They can play an important role in helping alleviate a major source of misery for people and communities.

As a licensed counselor of alcoholics and drug addicts, I encourage my clients to become involved in some kind of spiritual program. Counseling, in and of itself, has limited effectiveness. Client and therapist need a source of strength and discipline that surpasses the bounds of either and is available outside an agency's walls. Addicts need a place in which to make a lifelong and life-changing commitment to God and to one another. Unlike therapy, that place is something the church can offer. It is the purpose of this book to help the church and its leaders better understand and care for those who struggle with addictive problems.

---

1. Caroline Knapp, "The Glass Half Empty," *The New York Times Magazine* (9 May 1999): 19.

2. Jean Kinney and Gwen Leaton, *Loosening the Grip: A Handbook of Alcohol Information* (St. Louis: Mosby Press, 1995), 21.

3. Patrick Zickler, "Teen Drug Use Drops Slightly," *NIDA Notes* 14, no. 1 (1999): 8.

1

The Nature of Addiction

A lawyer once asked my opinion of one of her clients. Steve[1] was a business executive who had driven his car off the road and registered a .23 blood-alcohol concentration (BAC) on a police Breathalyzer. He was facing a DWI charge and the possibility of a fine and mandatory treatment. The lawyer thought the possible sentence was unnecessary since Steve was not an alcoholic; he was a corporate vice president with many responsibilities and earned several hundred thousand dollars a year. The accident was a single instance of poor judgment and did not merit marring his record. What symptoms would a counselor use to diagnose Steve's alcoholism?

After explaining the clinical traits, I pointed out that a .23 blood-alcohol reading was very high and might indicate a problem. To reach that level, Steve had to drink the equivalent of thirteen beers in a two-hour period and would remain legally drunk for seven hours after quitting.[2] On the one hand, those are not signs of a strictly social drinker. Many people could not walk to the car after consuming that much alcohol, let alone attempt to drive. On the other hand, one occasion of very poor judgment does not mean a person is an alcoholic. As Steve's lawyer knew, the criteria for alcohol dependence are broad, any symptom by itself proves little, and a diagnosis is based upon interpretation of the evidence.

Even though addiction is reviled as a societal disease, its definition is surprisingly vague. And that vague definition is the reason that many people have difficulty recognizing the presence of alcoholism or addiction. There are different perspectives for defining the disorder, and many misconceptions exist. In this chapter we will examine misconceptions and definitions of addiction, arriving at a method for identifying those who abuse alcohol and drugs.

MISCONCEPTIONS

A man using a lawyer to defend himself against being clinically diagnosed with a disease captures the ambiguous nature of addiction in American society. Addiction is regarded as both a deviant behavior and a biological illness. It is treated as a genetic condition, but also as chosen conduct. An addict is just as likely to end up in prison as in a clinic. No other pathology elicits such a culturally conflicted response. As a result, one misconception is that there is a clear definition or understanding of the problem.

The primary reason for the ambiguity in defining addiction is that addiction originated as a social problem, rather than as a medical one; social values are the underlying basis for determining its presence. Drinking or drug use that is common in some cultures may be categorized as abusive or addictive in ours. For example, patterns of vodka drinking in Russia are regarded as inappropriate in America, which leads to the reports that many Russian leaders are alcoholics, even though the Russians do not seem bothered by their alcohol consumption. The use of mescaline and peyote in some Native American communities is traditional and considered sacred; according to U.S. laws, these Native Americans are drug abusers and criminals. In France and Germany, it is not illegal to serve wine or beer to children during a meal; in America, it could get a person arrested.

The cultural values involved in determining drug or alcohol abuse indicate the importance of context in the definition. Addiction cannot be determined other than contextually.

Maladaptive patterns of use require a setting in which such patterns can be delineated and recognized.

However, within American society, there are different ideas about what type of substance use is maladaptive, what causes the maladaptive use, and how best to deal with it. Even professionals in the field have disagreements that at times are profound. Unanimity does not exist, and we often vacillate between different perspectives about addiction. Detecting our fluctuating opinions and achieving a clearer point of view are major goals of this chapter.

This current ambiguity concerning addiction leads to a second misconception. Like Justice Stevens defining pornography—"I know it when I see it"—people think they know an addict when they see one. The stereotype is a bum with a bottle in a bag, huddled on a sidewalk. That is the image the lawyer had in mind when she defended Steve by referring to his social position and accomplishments. Because he was a high achiever, she argued, Steve could not be an alcoholic. Another common stereotype is of a person who drinks a great deal every day. Evaluated by substance abuse clinicians, addicts frequently profess their health by declaring that they do not drink that often or that much. "I drink only in the evening . . . on weekends . . . at the club." "I never drink booze." "Three beers and I'm looped."

But these conceptions are misleading. People can be mistaken about the alcoholics or drug addicts they see, and frequently they do not see the ones with whom they interact everyday. For example, it is estimated that 95 percent of problem drinkers are either employed or employable.[3] Not everyone who is homeless or destitute is a drinker or drug abuser; not everyone who appears to be a drinker has a drug problem. People who achieve various measures of success, who fulfill responsibilities, who maintain families and go to church, may have addictive problems.

Similarly, addiction and abuse cannot be determined by social sectors, groups, or gender. Man or woman, professional or laborer, senior citizen or child, a member of Hell's

Angels or a regular churchgoer, and even clergy: addiction crosses all boundaries. One of the most severe alcoholics I ever treated had been a decorated state trooper who eventually found himself homeless on the streets of the state capital, divorced, estranged from his daughter, and receiving handouts from former colleagues.

Similarly, we cannot discount substance abuse among the elderly and the young. Retired persons, surviving spouses, and senior citizens often suffer from loneliness and boredom. Alcoholism, especially, can become an issue, even when it was not a problem earlier in life. On the other end, I counseled youths as young as eleven for drug abuse and had clients who began drinking and taking drugs in grade school.

We should not assume that addiction is more prevalent in men. While more men than women are accepted into treatment, and more rehabilitation facilities exist for men, men are not genetically more susceptible. Gender prevalence has more to do with cultural roles. Women who are diagnosed as addicted face a stronger social stigma, making them less likely to pursue help or admit a problem. Being an educated career woman does not obviate the possibility that she may be addicted to substances; however, it will be more emotionally expensive to her and entail greater social risk to accept treatment.

Similarly, we cannot assume that addiction is more likely found among residents of the inner city, or less likely found among those living in more affluent areas. Inner cities receive the brunt of law enforcement efforts, which are subsequently reported by the media, encouraging the stereotype. But drug deals are as readily transacted in suburban high schools, among people with more money to spend, as they are on city streets.

Obviously appearances can be deceptive when attempting to determine if someone is an alcoholic or addict. Unfortunately, except in extreme cases, medical symptoms are not much more helpful. There are no disease agents in blood tests that can identify the presence of addiction.

Despite some evidence that addiction may run in families, there are no genetic markers. And although a person can be tested for the presence of drugs or alcohol, a positive test does not necessarily mean the person is addicted. People do experiment or engage in occasional use. By the time medical evidence that indicates substance abuse emerges, permanent physical damage may already have occurred. Cirrhotic livers, esophageal lesions and hemorrhages, overdoses, drug-induced psychoses, heart attacks, impotence, and infertility can be the results of chronic drug and alcohol use. Although the hope is to intervene before these occur, imprecise symptoms and deceptive appearances make early intervention difficult.

The ambiguity of addiction also requires us to dispel our faith in explanations. We often think it is crucial to understand a problem's inner dynamics, to explain "why," before we feel ready to deal with that problem. But the importance of explanations is another misconception. The needs of addicts do not allow the reassurance of understanding them first.

As of now, addiction is not a disorder that can be explained. Its etiology is very unclear, if not still unknown. Studies in brain chemistry and genetics hope to pinpoint how addiction functions or originates, but these studies are biased toward a particular viewpoint and a particular perspective and have their own limitations. It is not unfair to say that addiction remains a mystery.

A good example is Claire. She was a forty-five-year-old, highly intelligent divorcee with two children in their early twenties. Claire had two years of college education and an artistic flair, and had worked in the past as an art restorer. She was also on probation for drug possession. When she came to me, she had been kicked out of a halfway house for drinking, was using her welfare check to rent a room at the YWCA, and was afraid she would be returned to jail for violating the terms of her release. Still, on her first day in the clinic I had to send her home because she was drunk. Initially

I thought she had used mouthwash to mask the smell of alcohol on her breath; later I learned that mouthwash was what she had been drinking.

In the past, Claire had seriously abused marijuana, cocaine, and hallucinogens. But alcohol was her drug of choice, and it was killing her. Her liver was enlarged and threatening failure. She repeatedly told me she did not want to die. She also wanted to contact her children, whom she had not seen in over a year because of her binge drinking, incarceration, and time spent in rehabilitation. However, despite the dangers of going back to jail, not seeing her children, and death, Claire was unable to stop drinking.

She could remain sober for five or six days. Then she would visit a man she knew who always had liquor in his apartment, and drink for a day or two. If he was not home, she would visit a grocery store and drink several bottles of mouthwash while pretending to shop. Finally, in desperation, she took a bus to her parents' home, hoping to get a fresh start some place safe. Her mother called me, looking for emergency advice. Although the mother had tried to remove all alcohol from the house, Claire had found a bottle of rubbing alcohol, which she drank.[4]

This kind of severe, nearly suicidal behavior is impossible to understand fully. It is not a problem of intelligence because in order to survive, addicts must be fairly intelligent. This woman did not lack incentives for recovery nor did she lack people who cared about her. There was a lot at stake, and she knew it. Her parents were not heavy drinkers. A variety of psychological causes might be suggested, after subjecting Claire to analysis, but they would be nothing more than conjectures and possibilities. Carl Jung, the famous psychiatrist, found alcoholism impossible to treat. A modern researcher might say that the brain's pleasure center was dominating the cerebral cortex. But pleasure had long ceased to be a driving force; misery was her common state.

Claire's severe alcoholism exemplifies the way addiction can defy explanation. Accepting the unexplainable is important for grasping addiction's nature. To recognize addiction and deal with addicts requires becoming comfortable with irrational behavior and not indulging a desire to make it all sensible.

The final misconception concerns the possible criminal or moral issues involved in addiction. Using an unlawful substance is not, in itself, a sign of addiction. There are people who use illegal drugs—pot being the most obvious example—in a social manner.[5] Many pot smokers smoke occasionally and in a manner that would not qualify them by any clinical criteria as addicted, other than the fact that using marijuana puts them in legal jeopardy. There is a tendency among authorities and clinicians to presume that anyone using illegal substances has a problem. But that assumption clouds the issue. A person could need counseling or intervention because of a willingness to break the law, and not for an addiction to substances. In terms of addiction itself, illegality is of secondary importance.

Sam was a middle-aged truck driver who worked for a local gravel pit. He had a good employment record, took care of his family, and had no criminal record. But he liked to sniff cocaine once or twice a month on weekends. His company gave drug tests to its employees, and Sam recorded a positive test for cocaine. He had sniffed on Saturday night and was tested on Monday morning. Since cocaine stays in a person's system for two to three days, he was caught. This did not mean he was high on cocaine when driving his truck. Since cocaine is illegal, however, he was mandated to counseling in order to keep his job and was told that another positive test would lead to his dismissal.

If Sam had used alcohol with the same frequency that he used cocaine, he would never have been forced into treatment. Instead, he would be regarded as a light drinker. Metabolized in a matter of hours rather than days, alcohol would not have shown up in a test taken one or two days later. Since alcohol is legal, his employer might not care if Sam is drunk all weekend, as long as he is sober by Monday.

In a case like this, a drug's illegality confuses the issue of whether a person abuses drugs. The legal ramifications create an abuse issue because of the consequences potentially suffered if the user is caught, even if a person's use might not otherwise have negative repercussions. Sam's counseling inevitably focused on the use of cocaine because of its illegality, not because of the manner in which he used it.

His case also highlights the similar confusion that can be caused by moral concerns. There is a difference between a person who uses a drug abusively and someone who uses a drug considered morally wrong. Some churches and religious communities have strong prohibitions against the use of any psychoactive substances, but members who do use are not necessarily addicted. Clergy must be able to put aside their moral beliefs temporarily in order to deal effectively with the individual. The morality of drug or alcohol use can be considered separately. Never is it more important to withhold judgment than when the church wishes to identify and help addicts. A whiff of judgment is frequently enough to drive already secretive people even deeper into hiding.

The conflicted attitudes and beliefs in American culture concerning addiction make misconceptions almost inevitable. Releasing these prevalent, but false, presumptions will enable us to perceive more accurately those who do genuinely suffer from drug abuse and addiction. We can turn our attention from what addiction is not to what it is.

CLINICAL CRITERIA

The guitarist Dickey Betts, a founding member of the Allman Brothers Band, was expelled from the band mid-tour during the summer of 2000. The band's press release said that Betts had "personal and musical differences" with the other musicians. The underlying allegation, however, was that Betts's drug and alcohol abuse was affecting his playing—he would lose the beat, play out of tune, or play the wrong song entirely. Gregg Allman told a reporter, "It's amazing how one person's disease can affect the band so much." Added to the band members' charges were Betts's two arrests in recent years, once for being abusive to his wife while he was drunk and a second for allegedly putting a gun to her head.

Dickey Betts, for his part, was taking the band to court, attempting to stop the tour. Disputing the band's claims, Betts insisted that he was not out of control: "I'm not strung out on any drugs; I'm not abusing alcohol." He said that he did not even keep beer on his tour bus. He was simply living the life of a rock and roll musician. "I'm a rock and roll guitar player. I've been arrested for being rowdy. I drink. I've had people come in the room with girls all over the place. But you're talking over a thirty-year period. That's part of rock and roll."[6]

If it were up to us to arbitrate this quarrel and determine whether the guitarist truly had a substance abuse problem, how would we go about it? What would be our criteria? What are reliable signs of drug abuse or alcoholism?

A clinical therapist, if asked to do an assessment, would use the symptoms for substance dependence set forth in the fourth edition of the *Diagnostic and Statistical Manual of Mental Disorders of the American Psychiatric Association (DSM-IV)*. The seven given criteria form the basis for diagnoses that are accepted throughout the mental health, social service, and criminal justice systems. The codification of these symptoms, which have been modified by the psychiatric association over the last twenty years, is an attempt to create an objective national standard based upon medical observation. To qualify as substance dependent, someone like Dickey Betts would have to display three out of the seven diagnostic symptoms. We'll examine each one.

1. Tolerance

Anyone who drinks on a regular basis learns, in time, that he or she may no longer be a cheap drunk. The body develops resistance to the effects of alcohol. The person who brags about being able to "hold my liquor" is describing not some aspect of machismo, but a normal physical adjustment found in those who drink more than occasionally. The *DSM-IV* gives two definitions of tolerance: a need for markedly increased amounts of a substance to achieve intoxication, or markedly diminished effects with continued use of the same amount. In practical terms, those two definitions describe the same thing: The drinker needs more to get a "buzz."

Tolerance is what accounts for the staggering amounts of alcohol some can consume. I have had clients whose blood-alcohol concentration (BAC) when arrested was three to four times the legal limit—levels that would leave most people unconscious or dead. Such a person, like the business executive, Steve, might register a .23 alcohol content on a Breathalyzer and not feel intoxicated. One alcoholic complained to me about being arrested with a BAC slightly over .1; he could not see how his abilities were impaired at that level.

Tolerance also develops with the use of other drugs, such as marijuana, heroin, and amphetamines. In the case of heroin and amphetamines, tolerance leads to using increasingly larger amounts to achieve the same effect, with the accompanying danger of an overdose. While one marijuana joint, or "blunt," may fail to get a person as high as it once did, smoking more is not the answer.[7] After the maximum high is achieved, smoking more pot is essentially wasteful. Addicts who smoke marijuana every day, all day ("24-7," in common parlance), do it mostly for show and are squandering a lot of money. But pot users rarely overdose on pot alone.

For obvious reasons, tolerance is used as a measure of addiction. In order to achieve tolerance, a significant quantity of alcohol or a drug must be regularly used. As tolerance increases, the quantities consumed and the time spent in consumption tend to grow, too, which may indicate current or potential problems. Large, regular amounts of a drug eventually interfere with a person's health, just as the time and money required will eventually cause problems at home, at work, and with finances. It is hard to ingest large amounts of certain chemicals without ultimately encountering negative consequences, and tolerance leads people into that kind of use.

When evaluating a possible addict, a clinician will try to get a sense of the amount of the drug used. When guitarist Betts drinks, how much does he drink—two to three beers, two to three six-packs, or a case and a half (thirty-six beers)? We must remember, however, that tolerance to the effects of a drug proves little by itself. A person can be a heavy drinker, smoke marijuana regularly, and even inject heroin without clinically being an addict. Other criteria are needed to corroborate what tolerance would seem to indicate someone's abuse of alcohol or drugs.

2. Withdrawal

When someone uses large amounts of chemicals and then quits, he or she feels aftereffects. A hangover is the most common example of withdrawal, and the second symptom cited in the *DSM-IV*. For clinical purposes, withdrawal can mean the manifestation of characteristic withdrawal symptoms or use of a drug in order to avoid withdrawal symptoms.

Drugs induce different types of withdrawal. The image of a heroin addict going "cold turkey" is one example. Withdrawal from opiates is highly unpleasant. Chills, sweats, muscle cramps, aching bones, diarrhea—heroin users will go through various tortures to get clean. The worst aspect may be the insomnia, which can last for weeks. For all the pain, however, heroin withdrawal is not life threatening.

Alcohol withdrawal, on the other hand, can be life threatening. Detoxification facilities exist primarily for the medical treatment of alcoholics in withdrawal because of the danger of fatal seizures. The mortality rate for untreated alcoholics undergoing withdrawal is somewhere between 8 and 24 percent.[8] Visiting a detox ward can be an unforgettable experience. Seeing alcoholics with such a severe case of the shakes that they cannot walk without leaning against the wall or who feel like something is crawling all over their skin is enough to make you temporarily question that glass of wine at dinner. These are the more developed symptoms of a hangover and usually indicate a case of high tolerance as well.

Although the withdrawal symptoms associated with marijuana and cocaine are more subtle, they do exist. Chronic pot smokers whose use is interrupted will frequently feel restless, irritable, and stressed. Chronic cocaine users will suffer primarily from an inability to feel normal levels of pleasure, clinically known as anhedonia. This symptom is caused by the manner in which cocaine alters brain chemistry and is a condition that can last for years. Crack smokers also manifest an intense irritability when "crashing," a term for withdrawal that speaks for itself.[9] This extreme irritability is the primary cause of violent crime associated with crack use.

Withdrawal can be so unpleasant that it becomes a compelling reason for many alcohol and drug abusers to continue using or to relapse if they try to quit, which is why the *DSM-IV* regards drug use to avoid withdrawal symptoms as a sign of withdrawal itself. When Jim Morrison of the band The Doors sang, "Woke up this morning and got myself a beer," he was describing a classic pattern for alcoholics throughout the world. Alcohol in the morning can forestall withdrawal effects. Careful alcoholics make sure they have a beer or two left in the refrigerator. One country-western singer who died of alcoholism would take a bottle of booze with him to bed to make sure he would have an "eye-opener" when he awoke.

Again, it is important to remember that withdrawal symptoms alone do not indicate addiction or abuse. Even tolerance and withdrawal together are not enough to substantiate a diagnosis. A person could drink a twelve-pack of beer at night, have another beer in the morning to relieve the shakiness, and not enter treatment if no other problems appeared. Although tolerance and withdrawal are often considered stereotypic signs of alcohol and drug abuse, they are not enough to make a diagnosis.

It is important, however, to understand the type of withdrawal symptoms a person may experience and their severity. Taking an alcohol or heroin addict to a detox ward may be necessary and even lifesaving.

3. Exceeding Intentions

When I was a teenager, there was a commercial for indigestion medication that showed a man, in obvious distress, expressing disbelief: "I can't believe I ate the whole thing." People with addiction problems frequently have similar experiences. Many times they have no intention of drinking or using any drugs, or, at least, not what they ultimately do. The lack of control over alcohol or drug activities is the third symptom detailed by the DSM-IV: The substance is often taken in larger amounts or over a longer period than was intended.

One of the hardest facts for addicts to accept is that they lack control. It does not seem reasonable to them that a desire to drink or drug can take over their behavior, even when they have strong desires to abstain. But people in the grip of an active addiction cannot trust themselves; they cannot trust their own thoughts, feelings, or best intentions. Most alcoholics and drug addicts test themselves, trying to drink or drug in a moderate manner. "Just a beer or two," they tell themselves, only to see that number escalate to another binge. People with several DWIs, who know they face prison if caught again, still find that their fear of punishment cannot keep their drinking within limits. They did not intend to exceed the legal limit when they walked in the bar, but they had exceeded it by the time they walked out.

The same dynamic is at work in regard to the time involved in use. Joe may have intended to be home in time for dinner when he stopped by for a beer; instead, he arrived four hours later to an angry spouse and children already in bed. Marijuana addicts are often unaware of the time they spend smoking pot and being high. Years can go by, and they will accomplish very little. That was not their plan, but the plan kept getting postponed while they "blazed."

The First Step of Alcoholics Anonymous emphasizes the addict's powerlessness against drug and alcohol use. One client told me that he had front-row seats to a Rolling Stones concert but missed the show because he drank through the entire weekend. All he could say was, "I don't know what happened." Addicts can go years not knowing what happened.

4. Failed Attempts to Quit

By the time people end up in a treatment facility, talking to someone like me, they have usually concluded that they have a problem. They have tried to quit many times. One seventeen-year-old, referred to me for smoking pot and drinking underage, had managed to abstain for six months the previous year. Failing tenth grade made him see that his drug use was interfering with his life. Unfortunately he was unable to sustain his drug-free lifestyle and failed tenth grade again. Faced with repeating tenth grade for the third time, he claimed to have seen the light. However, he returned to smoking pot every day and gave up entirely on school.

Treatment facilities are filled with chronic relapsers: people who repeatedly attempt to quit, only to fail. It is not unusual to have patients who have been in and out of treatment ten times or more. They know the counseling routine, have little new to learn about recovery, and have heard it all before. It is tempting to judge them as those who do not try or do not care.

However, frequent relapsing is the truest sign of addiction. No other symptom more clearly reveals its hold on people and their behaviors, and none is harder for nonaddicts to understand. To believe that a certain behavior is harmful and must be changed, for whatever reason—angry family, a lost job, possible incarceration, possible death, misery—and to return to that behavior is a demonstration of addiction in its starkest form.

Jeffrey was an accountant with wealthy clients, a large income, and a severe alcohol problem. He had already suffered three esophageal hemorrhages, caused by the caustic action of alcohol on the membranes of his throat. When an alcoholic suffers a hemorrhage, he or she can bleed to death quickly; Jeffrey was lucky to be alive. Our meeting was the latest of a string of inpatient rehabilitations. He was not an easy client because he literally knew it all. He knew the dangers of alcoholism and the methods that sustain abstinence. But I was not surprised to read his obituary in the newspaper several months after his discharge. I have no doubt that he started drinking again, despite what he knew.

Such an incident makes reasonable people want to shout, "Just say no!" "Just don't do it." They ask, "What are you thinking?" "Are you stupid?" "Don't you care?" But the only answer is they are addicted. This powerlessness is what the term addiction truly means.

5. Poor Use of Time

As tolerance and the amount an addict consumes increases, the amount of time required to maintain the habit increases commensurately. The lives of the severely addicted revolve around drug use, which leaves no time for other activities and interests. Boundaries are crossed even though the addict might have never thought it possible.

It is important to recognize that an addiction requires more time than is spent using drugs or being intoxicated. Time is needed to obtain whatever substance is being used and to recuperate. Time is spent while distracted by thoughts about using and by anticipating the next session. As addiction develops, addicts are increasingly unavailable to those around them, which is the primary cause of relationship stress, family breakdowns, and lost employment.

Studies indicate that substance abusers are late to work three to fourteen times more often than employees who do not abuse drugs. They are five to seven times more likely not to show up at all and three to four times more likely to be absent for longer than eight consecutive days.[10] These figures do not indicate laziness but time management problems. Greg, a factory worker, alcoholic, and crack smoker, was a typical case of using time poorly. He regularly showed up late to work or phoned in sick, depending on how he was feeling after drinking and smoking the previous night. He also arrived home later than his family expected, spending hours in a bar. Telling himself that he would be in time for dinner, he would stop for a beer and then spend the evening drinking, often smoking crack, and picking up a prostitute some nights. His wife was becoming increasingly frustrated. Chores around the house were not getting done, and he was a stranger to his children. He was risking being fired from his job. He stayed in treatment for about a week and checked himself out, saying he didn't have the time.

6. Interfering with Important Roles and Activities

The sixth clinical criterion of the *DSM-IV* states, "Important social, occupational, or recreational activities are given up or reduced because of substance use."[11] Because of the time required by substance use and addiction, impaired functioning, and personality changes, an addict is unable to maintain his or her social roles. When a person's accepted roles are not met because of drug use, a problem is indicated.

This symptom gets at the heart of addiction as a social problem. Public health concerns, in general, first arose in the eighteenth century as a response to a diseased and unreliable labor force. Increased productivity and lower costs of production associated with a healthy population are what make treatment for any addiction cost-effective in a capitalist society. Today's interest in addiction is an outgrowth of this original issue, and this clinical symptom is its clearest echo. In fact, since the government estimates that alcohol and drug abuse costs U.S. businesses more than $130 billion a year, an impaired labor force may remain the driving force of the laws, treatment, and research that address addiction.

However, the increasingly complex social structures of modern society have broadened the effects of substance abuse to other cultural roles. We specifically identify social and recreational activities. Everything from parent and spouse, to member of a softball team, to chair of the local PTA falls under this umbrella. Has alcohol or drug use diminished one's capacity to fulfill tasks or commitments?

This problem is, in part, a matter of boundaries. As the addiction progresses, substance use interferes with normal behaviors and responsibilities. Not only are addicts late to work, but also they are late picking up their spouses at the grocery store. Not only do they fail to show up at work, but also they fail to arrive at the committee meeting. While alone in their cars and on the way to accomplish tasks, addicts find the time ideal to "light up a bowl of pot." Once high, they lose interest, lose track of time, get paranoid, and prepare excuses for explaining their lapse. While there were probably times when they would not have allowed this to happen, either out of a sense of responsibility or of care, that sense has dissipated. Carelessness increases as responsibility wanes. This is the point at which users are more likely to get caught.

Of course, who cares if a person quits the softball team to stay home and drink beer, instead of staying on the team and drinking beer after the game? Whose business is it if an addict annoys his wife by forgetting to buy groceries because he was smoking marijuana? A man having an affair might do the same thing, but adultery is not regarded as a form of mental illness. Are quitting the softball team and forgetting to buy groceries signs of abuse or addiction? Alone, they are not. Addiction is indicated only when corroborated by other symptoms.

However, cultures concerned with addiction are correspondingly concerned with order. For example, as roles become more specific and the potential for disorder grows, anything that seriously interrupts patterned interactions is likely to be regarded as pathological. Pathological behaviors do not have a predictable product and so are poor investments. The diagnosis and treatment of mental illness and addiction have risen together in Western societies. So it is fair to say that without this particular symptom, none of the others would arouse much anxiety or interest.

7. Making Problems Worse

Some people have medical or psychiatric problems that have been either caused or made worse by the use of alcohol and drugs. When people know this fact and continue to drink and drug, they exhibit the final symptom presented by the *DSM-IV*. As might be expected, they are often the saddest cases.

Deborah was a single mother with three school-aged children and working for a temporary placement agency. She could barely make ends meet in the best of circumstances and could only afford an apartment in the poorest part of the community. Added to this grinding existence was her diagnosis of clinical depression, which she admitted was accurate. However, she refused to accept psychiatric treatment or medication. Instead, she compensated with an aggressive, rebellious attitude and used pot and beer as substitute medications.

Deborah understood that both alcohol and marijuana are sedatives that would make her depression worse. But she claimed not to care. When a stint on probation made her quit smoking pot, she simply drank more. She had no involvement with a spiritual community and no connection to a God in whom she could find hope. Her growing depression dragged her deeper into debt, causing her family to move to the most dangerous part of the city. She allowed men to use her and allowed her apartment to be used as a flophouse. Meanwhile, she continued to proclaim that she would do as she pleased. To watch an intelligent woman destroy her family and herself was difficult. Occasionally she would admit to the deepening depression and downward spiral and negative effects of her drug use, but she still refused to change. Deborah is an example of a person displaying this final symptom. Many mentally ill persons will abuse street drugs, which interfere with their prescribed medications and exacerbate their illness, just as people with cirrhotic livers will continue to drink and people with high blood pressure will continue to smoke crack. Showing no regard for their own well-being by continuing to consume drugs is a sure sign of a serious problem, often indicative of people who simply do not care anymore.

ABUSE VERSUS ADDICTION

The *DSM-IV* creates a secondary category of substance abuse, distinct from the diagnosis of addiction. Abuse, in the manual, refers to a less developed situation in which alcohol or drug use has caused a recurrent problem of some kind but the overall circumstances do not rise to the level that would qualify someone as addicted. For example, if a person has more than one DWI or gets into repeated arguments with his or her spouse when drinking, and does not meet all the criteria for alcoholism, then a diagnosis of abuse is warranted.

The essential point in this distinction is that problems with substance use cover a wide spectrum of severity. In that sense, addiction in the *DSM-IV* is a term describing the condition of someone for whom the negative consequences of drug use have branched out and are interfering with several aspects of life, rather than one or two. By the same measure, a person who demonstrates a recurring problem of any kind associated with drinking or drugging still has just that—a problem.

It is not unreasonable to expect that many who abuse drugs may someday be addicted to drugs. Unless there is intervention, substance abuse has a tendency to get worse rather than better. This pattern is known as progression and is one of the ways that addiction can resemble a disease. The quantities used and frequency of use increase; the types of drugs change; the associated problems become more serious and chronic.

Bill had been referred to me by his probation officer. Convicted of assault for breaking someone's jaw during a drunken brawl, he was under a court order not to drink. A result of this order, however, was that he began to smoke pot more frequently. Being a very tense and emotionally constricted young man who used drugs to relax, Bill found that pot worked even better than alcohol, because alcohol was likely to send him into a rage. Despite the danger of incarceration for violating probation, he had difficulty staying drug-free. Bill finally managed to achieve three months without smoking pot after a year of counseling, but he was back in treatment six months later. He was drinking and smoking pot again, and he had begun to sniff cocaine. He lost his girlfriend because of his verbal abusiveness. In a span of three years, Bill had progressed from abusing one drug to abusing three, in a manner that cost him significant relationships and threatened to put him back in jail. And there was no reason to believe that his progression had come to an end.

A PRACTICAL METHOD

As helpful as the diagnostic criteria can be for suggesting the types of problems that accompany substance abuse and addiction, they are also unwieldy. Trying to keep in mind seven different symptoms while conversing with someone, then reviewing that person like a checklist to see if three or more were achieved, can seem both awkward and artificial. Concentrating on the symptoms may end up interfering in a conversation that is meant to be more narrative and personal than inquisitorial.

The *DSM-IV*'s two classes of addiction and abuse also encourage a categorization of people that does not always reflect reality. Fitting people into such a taxonomic table risks overlooking important nuances of their characters and actions. The complexity of someone's life, and even of his or her substance abuse, is not adequately summarized by a label or by a twofold category that often renders a false sense of having determined the problem. One of the important gifts a religious community has to offer is a clinical-free approach to people.

Using these criteria as background, I suggest a more direct, practical, and personal method. The primary reason to stop using alcohol or drugs is their interference in a person's life. As the *DSM-IV* symptoms suggest, negative consequences or interference can occur in many different areas, from the legal to the medical to the relational, as well as exacerbate other problems. These consequences, then, are the signs for which we look. Is substance use interfering with how a particular person lives his or her life? Are there certain patterns to the interference? Do some consequences tend to repeat? Interference is the issue, regardless of the label it is given, and is the most practicable way to search for possible abuse.

In a conversation with Steve, the business executive, we may learn that he never had a DWI or other alcohol-related problem before. At a retirement party for a friend, he overdrank and struggled to get in his car. He fell asleep in the driver's seat before starting the engine. He had intended to sleep it off, not realizing he could be arrested just for sitting behind the wheel when drunk. In such a case, lacking a pattern of trouble, Steve could not be said to have a substance abuse problem, even with his DWI. A discussion is warranted, however, about the risk of his poor decision. Even though he did not drive, he could have fallen over on the front seat when he was passed out, regurgitated, and then drowned in his own vomit. Many people, including several rock-and-roll celebrities, have died in exactly that manner.

On the other hand, we may learn that although Steve has only one DWI, there have been other evenings when he drove under the influence of alcohol. On Friday nights after work, he usually stopped at a club for cocktails before heading home. Since his home is only two miles away, he figures he can manage the trip; indeed, he has done so on other nights. It is fairly common, in fact, for someone with a DWI to have driven drunk many times without being caught. His prior experiences of driving home safely have led Steve to feel slightly annoyed at being stopped, believing the arrest is unjustified in his case. He is in control. Steve makes it clear that he had not planned to drink as much as he did. Things just got away from him a little, friends were buying drinks, and he ended up staying a couple of hours, drinking seven or eight bourbons.[12]

In this case, Steve's beliefs about his driving ability are an aspect of his denial. In order to justify his drinking and his willingness to place himself and others at risk, he must deny his impairment and poor decisions. In other words, drinking has displaced honesty and safety and led him to break the law routinely and knowingly. We should note that he shows a marked tolerance for alcohol and drank more than he planned. We might also learn that Steve's wife is not happy about his Friday nights at the club, partly because on Saturdays he is hungover for most of the day.

This is a pattern of behaviors and attitudes that indicate someone with a problem. In Steve's case, there are several ways that alcohol is interfering in his life: by breaking the law, putting himself in dangerous situations, placing a strain on his marriage, and taking over a great deal of his discretionary time. The most basic goal is to identify such interference in people. Regardless of their level of substance abuse, they need help in some way. They may become argumentative when drinking or fail to finish homework when smoking marijuana. They may overuse prescribed pain relievers or take them with alcohol. They may risk arrest, loss of job, and public humiliation in order to sniff cocaine on the weekend. Or the consequences may have become much worse.

In a following section, we will discuss helping someone admit that substance use is interfering in his or her life.

Interference in one's life is the most compelling and personal reason to consider quitting, and helping someone to admit his or her abuse is the first step in any successful intervention. But once that admission has been made, the next issue is whether quitting is even possible. Some people are able to put down the bottle of beer or pipe full of pot and not go back once they decide it is a problem. But many people, if not most, will not find the resolution that easy. They may abstain for a while, but in time they return to drinking or drugging, establishing a pattern of using interrupted by periods of respite, which progressively worsens.

Again, speaking practically, this is the mark of addiction as opposed to abuse. Many who admit their substance use is a problem will be unable to maintain abstinence or to use their drug in a more controlled manner. Eventually, they will drink or take drugs again as they did before, with the same problems, despite their best intentions. In the terminology of the Twelve Steps, they find themselves powerless to change their patterns of behavior. In that sense, addiction is a condition that truly becomes known in time. For such people, special help will be necessary.

OTHER ADDICTIONS

This view makes clear that addiction is not limited to the use of alcohol and drugs, considering addiction is a pattern of behavior that interferes with life and is not amenable to a person's efforts at self-control. Gambling is an obvious example. Gambling addiction leads to many of the same problems as drug and alcohol use, and chapters of Gamblers Anonymous exist to provide support based on the Twelve Steps.

Stephanie was married, articulate, and religious and came for treatment of a gambling problem. At one time she had been a crack addict, but had entered recovery and was now abstinent from drugs. While remaining drug-free, however, she developed an addiction to gambling that quickly grew out of control. Before long she was embezzling money from work, spending family funds earmarked for other needs, and running up large debts. This continued until her employer caught her stealing and had her arrested. While in counseling, she also identified an addiction to shopping. Her addiction was more serious than simply spending too much. If she did not gamble, she would visit a mall, literally shaking in anticipation, and spend large sums of money on stuff she did not need. As a result, she had extensive collections of various knick-knacks. It was a habit that, like gambling, led to debts, dishonesty, and serious marital trouble.

There are many such maladaptive patterns, most of which are not regarded as psychiatric problems at this time but do interfere with people's lives. Twelve Step groups exist for gambling, overeating, codependency, sexual addiction, and other maladies as well. Another likely candidate for a Twelve Step program is Internet addiction, for those who spend countless hours on-line, depriving themselves of sleep and damaging their relationships. I have read articles that discussed, only half-mockingly, being addicted to computerized card games. If we start to play them, we may taste what more serious addictions are like.

Another special case is addiction to tobacco products. Reviled as a health risk, but also heavily advertised and subsidized as a cash crop, tobacco exists in a cultural twilight zone of politics and economics. Nicotine makes quitting difficult by creating unpleasant withdrawal symptoms, even when medical problems make abstinence advisable. However, professional treatment and organized help are largely lacking.

The reason this book deals primarily with addiction to alcohol and other mood-altering chemicals is that they are the addictions our culture chooses to treat in a special manner, often punitively. Other addictions exist but do not receive the same social attention. They have their own unique difficulties but often lack recognition and support. For instance, gambling can be an addiction; it is also an activity used by various states to gain revenue. Shopping can be an addiction, but the media encourages us to spend. Even drug addiction is encouraged. We can say that addiction is an integral aspect of the way modern culture operates in America.

CAUSES

I have not included the possible causes of addiction for two reasons. One reason is that understanding addiction's etiology is not necessary to offer effective ministry. Many people succeed in recovery despite the fact that addiction remains largely a malady of mysterious origins. For all the advances in medical science, it is still impossible to explain why particular people become sick at certain times. When the flu passes through a community, why do some become ill with the virus and others do not? Why doesn't every smoker get lung cancer? For that matter, why do some people with a disease have unexplainable spontaneous remissions? Medicine can only offer statistics and probabilities, but that does not prevent the successful treatment of illness. It is no different with addiction.

Second, the various theories about the origins of addiction have yet to resolve the issue. Some points of view are strongly advocated in certain circles, which then lead to particular treatment approaches, but nothing is conclusive. Addiction is an aspect of human behavior, which remains irrational, mysterious, and an affront to a scientific perspective that believes everything must have a rational cause. One of the reasons that spirituality works so well with the addicted is that a spiritual perspective does not have that rationalistic shortcoming. We believe that mystery and irrationality are an important experience in life and that healing, as well as dysfunction, can arise from them. Religion transcends purely rational understandings.

For example, scientists have advanced genetic theories to explain addiction. A compelling study seeking a genetic link compared adopted children who had at least one alcoholic biological parent with adopted children whose biological parents were nonalcoholic. Using three subcategories (heavy drinker, problem drinker, and alcoholic), the study found that the male children of alcoholics were four times more likely to become alcoholics themselves. There were no differences between the females. Among those adopted sons of alcoholic biological parents, however, a majority (51 percent) still did not fall into any of the three subcategories and manifested no alcohol-related problems. In fact, a greater percentage of the adopted children of nonalcoholic biological parents (55 percent) fit into one of the three subcategories than did those whose parents were alcoholic (49 percent).[13] Perhaps the stress of being adopted is more predictive for problem drinking than genetic makeup.

The results of these studies are highly ambiguous, despite the confidence of some researchers that genes will be proved to account for most or all human behavior. For those who believe that the cause of alcoholism is in our chromosomes, the best hope for a cure lies in the manipulation of genetic structure, in an effort to remove inherited diseases from the human genome.[14]

All etiological theories, including those involving brain chemistry, family histories, cultural values, and psychological profiles, have similar ambiguities. Although these theories may designate groups of people statistically more at risk for developing addictive problems, none can specify which individuals will become addicts. Neither can etiological theories isolate common disease agents among addicts nor convincingly offer an underlying process to explain addiction. As such, neither can they develop cures for those who become addicted.

In reality, addiction does not have a single or primary cause, and most addicts probably have a variety of causes for their own habits. All or some theories may apply to any individual persons, including those addicted for no apparent reason, which helps account for the difficulty addicts experience in dealing with their dysfunction. An alcoholic may have a genetic predisposition, an alcoholic family environment, psychological needs addressed by drinking, and live in a culture in which people are more susceptible to alcoholism. Such an addict will have to address a number of factors in order to remain drug- and alcohol-free.

Part of the wisdom of the Twelve Steps is that etiology is not an issue. It does not matter why a person has the flaws that he or she does. All that matters is whether the person is dealing with those flaws. That is the lesson, in the Gospel of John, of the diseased man who had lain beside the pool called Bethesda for thirty-eight years. His healing began when he finally took some action. Religious communities are perfectly situated to help the addicted do the same.

---

1. All names used in this book are fictitious. All references to particular people have been altered in order to protect their identities.

2. A twelve-ounce beer, a four-ounce glass of wine, and a one-ounce glass of 86 proof whiskey are roughly equal in alcohol content. The federal definition of intoxication is a .08 blood alcohol concentration.

3. Jean Kinney and Gwen Leaton, *Loosening the Grip: A Handbook of Alcohol Information* (St. Louis: Mosby Press, 1995), 21.

4. I advised her to take Claire to the hospital, since drinking isopropyl alcohol can be fatal.

5. Pot, weed, hemp, herb, bud, grass, trees, and smoke are all common colloquialisms for marijuana.

6. Jenny Eliscu, "Dickey Betts: The Allmans' Lost Brother," *Rolling Stone* 846 (August 2000): 22.

7. The term "blunt" refers to a hollowed-out Phillies Blunt cigar filled with marijuana.

8. Darryl Inaba and William Cohen, *Uppers, Downers, All Arounders: Physical and Mental Effects of Psychoactive Drugs*, 2nd ed. (Ashland, Ore.: CNS Productions, 1993), 135.

9. Crack is a term for a distilled, cooked, and hardened form of cocaine sold as "rocks" or "bumpies" and commonly smoked in a small glass pipe. People who free-base cocaine make the same end product. Buying crack is a way to buy cocaine with the free-basing already done.

10. Inaba and Cohen, *Uppers, Downers, All Arounders*, 219.

11. *Diagnostic Ctiteria from DSM-IV* (Washington, D.C.: American Psychiatric Association, 1994), 109.

12. The body metabolizes the equivalent of approximately one can of beer per hour. This means that a person must drink five beers (.02 each) in

an hour to achieve the legal level of intoxication at .08 blood-alcohol level. This will vary by gender and size.

13. Peter Steinglass, *The Alcoholic Family* (New York: Basic Books, 1987), 296-97.

14. It is worth noting that these studies are conducted in regard to alcoholism, not with other drugs or other addictions. Whether heroin or gambling addictions demonstrate similar genetic links has not been investigated, nor whether they would have a different genetic code.

2

Helping the Addicted

Darryl Strawberry was a major-league baseball player whose career came to a premature end because of his addiction to cocaine. In a series of public fiascoes, which included numerous arrests, Strawberry has demonstrated how addicts can lose control of their lives. Once earning millions of dollars and basking in public acclaim, he reached a level of athletic success that few achieve and that might have taken him to the Hall of Fame. But he could not remain drug-free. He repeatedly returned to cocaine, and the consequences ruined him. Such self-destruction is always a tragic sight.

Part of the tragedy is that help is available. Having the monetary resources at his disposal, Darryl Strawberry has access to any type of treatment and therapy he chooses. He has friends and former employers offering support. Chapters of Narcotics Anonymous are found in most communities. Yet, as the press reports, he has failed to follow through: leaving rehab early, not attending support groups, returning to places that encourage dangerous behavior.[1] He appears not to care. That is probably an inaccurate assumption. Rather, he is demonstrating a fact that everyone who works with the addicted must accept: Recovering from addiction, for most people, is a long and winding road.

For those who are accustomed to dealing with addicts, Strawberry's actions are not especially surprising, nor are those of Robert Downey Jr., another celebrity addict who continues to find trouble. Their relapses are simply more public than those of many thousands of others who anonymously struggle in similar ways. Helping the addicted requires patience, honesty, a nonjudgmental attitude, and a carefully maintained willingness not to take addicts' failures personally. When one of my clients does well, I do not take that as proof of my therapeutic brilliance, just as I do not take their frequent slips and defeats as proof that I am poor at my work. It's an attitude, however, that I have had to develop and continually monitor.

One of the results of addiction's power is not only that it lies beyond the self-control of the afflicted person, but also that it lies beyond the control of any person, including those who desire to help. Addiction cannot be directed, issued ultimatums, threatened with hell or prison, or driven out. Addiction can only be loved. Of course, considering how poorly love is understood in our culture, much more needs to be said. But love is a good place to start. We cannot control others or make them change. We can only manage ourselves, and in managing ourselves is the basis for any therapeutic relationship. Below are several basic principles that will benefit anyone working with addicted people.

THERAPEUTIC POSITIONS

1. Patience

The description of love in 1 Corinthians 13 begins with this quality, which has proved to be very important to those in Alcoholics and Narcotics Anonymous. The slogan "One day at a time" is perhaps the most famous dictum encouraging patience. Another is, "Aim low, go slow, and achieve greatly." Addicts who succeed in recovery learn the hard way the dangers of attempting to move too quickly or take shortcuts. Neglecting or dealing with certain situations in a cursory manner, due to impatience, frequently leads to a relapse

42

and is the major reason recovery becomes a long road. Addicts learn they must be patient with themselves, their problems, and their healing.

The fable about the race between a rabbit and a tortoise is a useful one for addicts. The race, of course, is not won by the swift rabbit, but by the determined, careful, and persistent steps of the turtle. Having an impatient attitude does not work for those dealing with addiction because of the resulting carelessness and loss of focus. These are results that addicts cannot afford.

Those offering ministry cannot be impatient either. Expecting quick results from the addicted will most often frustrate those offering ministry and result in their losing interest. As mentioned earlier, it is not unusual to counsel people who have been in various forms of treatment many times. Very few addicts find recovery on their first attempt. Addicts will tell stories about people who were able to quit drinking or drugging without counseling or meetings. For people who struggle and must work very hard to establish a healthy life, such recoveries seem magical and are described with jealousy and wishful thinking. Most addicts who succeed in gaining control over their addiction are people who have demonstrated an impressive commitment to becoming well and who have picked themselves up, perhaps numerous times, from having fallen. In practical terms, effective ministry means hanging in there with them and providing a constant in a turbulent life.

Patience is also required when addicts manifest denials and delusions. There will be times when we wonder how anyone could fool himself or herself so completely. I counseled a man who had six DWIs and insisted that from then on he would control his drinking. I have counseled crack smokers who claimed finally to realize how much they needed help and then were unable to find a time to schedule appointments. I counseled a twenty-eight-year-old man who failed to finish high school, worked part-time at McDonald's, still lived with his parents, and played video games most of the day, who repeatedly denied that daily pot smoking was a problem. These are people who work very hard not to let reality interfere with their perceptions. In dealing with such people, patience is necessary while waiting until reality crashes the party, as it always does. Then we will have their ear, at least briefly.

2. Honesty

It is important for addicts to have a place where they can return without shame after a relapse, in order to begin again. But this should not be a place where failure is hidden or the true import of behaviors is deflected. Instead, it should be a place of reality without guilt and where people can find the courage to look at themselves. An atmosphere of honesty is important, especially for people who use dishonesty to survive.

In the book on the organization Alcoholics Anonymous, Bill Wilson makes clear that honesty is essential to recover from alcoholism. This is because dishonesty is a normal part of addicts' lifestyles. They routinely lie to themselves, as in denial, and to others.

I do not mean to imply that people with addictive problems are innately flawed or liars from birth. Rather, they are people who consider dishonesty expedient, almost required by their drug use. After all, many are doing something illegal, and even those who can legally drink probably have driven drunk or broken some other law while intoxicated. Admitting you smoke crack or shoot heroin is confessing to a crime.

Of course, there is much more to an addict's dishonesty than fear of the law. Addicted persons' denials and schemes require that others not know about the addiction, which places much importance on concealing the drug problem as long as possible. I have had clients doggedly refuse to admit using anything, despite having a positive drug test, and claim the results were mistaken or caused by something they ate; it is much easier to deny addiction with relatives and friends. Consequently, the addicted can become adept at maintaining a secret life, hiding money and drugs, concealing their drug paraphernalia and excursions to buy drugs. A highly successful financial consultant, who was also an alcoholic and crack addict, put it this way:

> Everybody was fooled. My wife didn't even know. My ex-wife now. She didn't even realize I was an alcoholic. I'd go drinking every night after work and go home, and she wouldn't know I'd been drinking. I had two DWIs, but I had a lot of money, so the first one I beat. The second one, I got reduced. . . . I was a master at the game. I was taught never to let somebody see you weak. Never let somebody see you down. Never show vulnerability because that's weakness, and you'll lose. So I think part of the problem with my family is that they had no clue. And as far as the perceptions of others . . . unless I went through what I went through I would not be able to understand it either. I mean, "How could you be a drug addict?" you know? And the answers that I provide for them today, half the time they believe I'm still not being honest with them. And half the time they really want to believe and understand, but they really can't.

As addiction progresses and the need for a drug increases, the pressure to find the required money and time also increases. This leads to even more dishonesty, as people lie to get what they crave. Schemes are created to ensure the necessary cash flow and drug availability. Lies hide the schemes, and then more lies make the previous lies seem plausible. Lying becomes a lifestyle, and addicts will often find themselves lying when it's not even necessary, until something brings down the whole house of cards. It is at this juncture of dishonesty and scheming that criminal activity is most likely to begin.

Establishing honesty, then, becomes essential in helping the addicted. In many ways, honesty goes to the heart of an addict's behaviors. In order to maintain a long-term abstinence from substance use, an addict must deal with more than merely not ingesting a drug and must address the peripheral behaviors that support that lifestyle. Something as seemingly simple as honesty strikes at the heart of an addict's denial, hiding, and scheming, without which his or her dysfunction cannot continue.

However, for many people, attempting to escape that manner of living and establishing a pattern of honesty will not be immediate achievements, which is why it is important for those offering care to initiate a relationship based on honesty from the beginning. The addicted are best served with straightforward feedback and a clear picture of the reality they avoid and have created; not to be honest with the addicted is a form of enabling.

An enabling dishonesty usually minimizes the seriousness of a situation and is motivated by a desire to avoid involvement. It may arise from wanting to sidestep hassles or not knowing what to do about a situation. In either case, avoidance is not helpful because it supports an addict's skewed perceptions. It is best to be direct, although not in a mean or judgmental manner, while understanding that there will be occasions when that direct approach is not justified. But those occasions should always be based on a compassion for the person in need rather than on our own discomfort.

3. Withholding Judgment

People with addictive problems often become involved in many other dysfunctional and socially unacceptable behaviors. The behaviors can occur because their desire for drugs leads them into risky activities and environments. The actions also occur because using alcohol and drugs changes the way they think. When inhibitions are lowered or ability to reason is diminished, trouble frequently follows.

Sally was an alcoholic and addicted to pain medication. She had married an alcoholic, with whom she had three children. When drinking, which was most of the time, the two adults engaged in violent arguments, which their daughter would attempt to stop. Eventually, the daughter talked with a school counselor about the fighting and about being raped by her father. An investigation revealed that the father had sexually abused his two sons as well. For the sexual abuse, the father was sentenced to prison for fifteen years. The children were removed from the home but allowed to visit Sally on the weekends, with the goal of returning to live with their mother. During one weekend visit, however, Sally got drunk and had sex with her youngest son. She did not remember the incident, but her son reported it. As a result, Sally lost all parental rights and never saw her sons again.

Sally's actions—abusing her son and failing to protect her children from their father—remain disturbing. But her actions were also directly connected to her drinking and drug use, which blinded Sally to what was happening around her and changed her into a woman filled with rage. As an active addict, she barely maintained control and, obviously, at times failed. Sally described the changes caused by her drug use in this way:

> When I'd get drinking I got more, like, violent. Pushy. I can remember a guy who wanted to dance with me, and I told him to get away from me because I was ready to punch him out. Because he was drunk, and there I am drinking, and he wants to dance with me, and I'd say "No thank you." And he wouldn't take a hint. A "no," and then I'd say "Leave me alone and get lost." I felt very powerful when I drank.

Even considering the effect of drugs on a person's personality and behaviors, not indulging in judgment can be difficult, especially when children are involved. Sally had been referred to our agency from another treatment center, in part because the previous staff just did not like her. But gaining a person's trust is essential when trying to help, and people are not likely to trust someone by whom they feel condemned. I have counseled all manner of criminals and sinners, and I have difficulty not judging those who have child after child, while lacking either the motivation or the ability to parent. When a man brags to me about having gotten a woman pregnant, after already having a series of children for whom he does little, my thoughts are not kind. But I will probably have little influence upon his behavior if I let those thoughts rule the relationship. Learning how to love the enemy can be a practical matter.

When dealing with those I find difficult to love, I make myself remember my own shortcomings and sins. There are people who have found me difficult to love, as well. Humility helps prevent indignation. I also choose not to react to the fears their behaviors arouse in me. Though I may think someone's actions despicable, my fears are my own problem. Allowing those fears into the relationship will only interfere, if ministry is the goal. Fear is what leads to judgment.

Withholding judgment creates the space to find a person's humanity. As reprehensible as I thought Sally's conduct was, she needed to be treated like any other fallible human being. In fact, she did well in treatment. In three years of counseling, she made remarkable progress, remaining abstinent from alcohol and drugs and attending AA meetings. She became involved in her church, taught Sunday school, volunteered at a local shelter, and re-established a positive relationship with her daughter. The last I knew, she had still not heard from either son, but she maintained hope that she would hear from them soon.

4. Maintaining Personal Boundaries

When I first entered the ministry, many of the mistakes I made resulted from the role I assumed as a rescuer. I still remember the time I asked a teenager to come see me. I knew there had been problems at home and thought she could use some help; of course, that was not necessarily what she thought. She came to my office with a quizzical look on her face. In response to my questions, she said she was doing fine and there were no problems at home, and so ended the discussion. It took me numerous similar experiences to learn that people have a right not to want help and need to be ready to receive it.

Jesus' response to the rich young man (Matt. 19:16-22) is instructive. When the man chose not to comply with Jesus' suggestion, he walked away, and Jesus let him go. Jesus did not run after him or try to convince him of the merit of his advice. Unlike that of many of us, Jesus' self-confidence was not linked to how people reacted to his work. He did not take their rejection or their failure to grow as a personal referendum and so was able to let people be. While he had an agenda, he didn't impose it. This unwillingess to pursue self-interest is the only way that God's presence in the world can be understood. The danger for the rest of us is that our boundaries are not as adequately maintained and our own interests become mixed with our concerns for the interests of others. The statement in 1 Corinthians 13—that love "does not seek its own"—is an important maxim in any pastoral or therapeutic relationship (v. 5 NASB).

Mixing our own concerns with the concerns for others can lead to trouble in two ways. The first way is that when someone, like an addict, does not follow through with our advice or guidance, we take his or her actions personally. We may question our abilities or become frustrated by the lack of visible results. Such unwarranted conclusions ultimately end in our own burnout. The turnover among counselors in the substance abuse field is high for this reason. The second, and perhaps more troublesome, issue is to end up supporting the behaviors of an addict by our attempts to help. In other words, we become enablers.

For example, it is very important not to protect the addicted from the consequences of their actions, even when those are heartbreaking to watch. Suffering consequences is the primary way that an addict concludes that he or she needs to quit or get help. Addicts will frequently talk about recognizing their problem by "hitting bottom," which generally describes having some kind of painful or frightening experience. Maybe hitting the bottom is getting arrested, becoming homeless, or spending all of their money. But these consequences can be deflected by family, friends, and others who intervene, in a spirit of concern. In the end, that kind of intervention is not helpful for the addict, even if it helps others feel useful or benevolent. Separating our own needs from the needs of those requiring help is necessary.

Sometimes these enabling interactions can be subtle. Ken was a crack addict who had a chronic history of relapses. He could manage to abstain for two or three months but would inevitably smoke again, usually in response to feeling angry and frustrated. He would feel guilty and ashamed afterwards and then find someone with whom he could share his self-disgust. His feelings, however, were self-pity and a substitute for taking action. Rather than learn other ways to handle his emotions, and then putting what he learned into practice, he would find fault with himself and give someone the opportunity to lend an enabling shoulder. In counseling, it was necessary to discuss how his self-defeating self-pity inadequately replaced taking responsibility for his behaviors.

Attempts to rescue people from themselves do not work, although addicts like to be rescued. Soon enough, the responsibility for keeping them straight becomes the rescuers' responsibility, not their own. If an addict used drugs, it's because someone was not by the phone to talk or did not get him or her to the AA meeting or was not sufficiently understanding. When that reversal of accountability takes place, when boundaries are not adequately maintained, little real help will occur.

ASSOCIATED PROBLEMS

By nature, addiction easily leads to many other problems. The term substance abuse indicates that negative consequences have been encountered, and these consequences are often extremely serious in their own right. As a result, the addicted rarely are helped for simply a drug problem. They bring with them a matrix of related troubles that interact with and exacerbate one another, so that effective ministry means dealing with a package of issues, connected through drug usage. Because of their frequency, a few encountered problems deserve special mention.

1. Medical Issues

A person cannot ingest large amounts of chemicals over a significant period of time without having adverse effects on his or her body. Addicts contract illnesses by both the drugs they use and the methods they utilize to get high. A significant percentage of addicts will be ailing, and the types of maladies will often be related to the types of drugs they are taking. As a rule, when dealing with someone who wants to get sober and become well, I strongly suggest that person also get examined by a doctor.

The primary concern, from the standpoint of ministry, is to be aware that medical issues may exist and need care in their own right. The behaviors of addicts can result in terminal diseases or permanent disability. Ministry, in those cases, will be concerned with more than drug use. The management of fatal illness and death is an area where a religious community has much more to offer than AA meetings or clinical treatment.

HIV and hepatitis C are two examples of diseases commonly found in addicts. Since both diseases are spread through contact with contaminated blood, drug users who inject the drug with a needle face a high risk of contracting either disease. Even though people who inject heroin might try to use only their own "works" or clean the hypodermic needle before sticking themselves, the reality is that often this does not happen. Cravings overtake reason, and when that occurs, addicts will use what is at hand. It takes only one shot with an infected needle to become another statistic with an incurable illness.

Similarly, many drug users engage in risky sexual behaviors. When high, they may become careless about using condoms. They may become prostitutes or use prostitutes. Either way, the end result can be many kinds of sexually transmitted diseases, including HIV and AIDS.

Other diseases result from the drugs themselves. Cirrhosis of the liver is the classic example, caused by the effects of chronic, heavy drinking. Since the liver bears the brunt of metabolizing alcohol, long-term abuse results in irreversible scarring and lesions, which may prove fatal. Excessive alcohol can also cause ulcers, upset hormone levels, and lead to high blood pressure. The drug cocaine raises the heart rate while constricting blood vessels, causing a sudden onset of high blood pressure, which can trigger cardiac collapse. The basketball player Len Bias is a recent example: he died at the age of twenty-two from cocaine intoxication.[2]

People dealing with the addicted will find that they need further education about these diseases. For example, not everyone is comfortable with people who are HIV positive. It is common to fear catching HIV by casual contact or to be uneasy about how individuals contracted it. But these are concerns a person needs to resolve before offering effective aid to the diseased. Most communities have resources for those with HIV, in particular, and offer educational opportunities to learn more about the illness.

These illnesses are a concern to counselors because of their direct effect upon the health of the infected individual and the emotions they produce. Someone who is HIV positive, or whose infection has progressed into AIDS, may struggle with feelings of hopelessness, which may make drug use more inviting. Depressed because they have a disease, they may not care anymore, even though drinking and drugging serve only to worsen their situation. The disease serves as a relapse trigger that then aggravates their disease. It's a cycle that a worker with the addicted can try to stop. Because of the medical advances that have been made, people with diseases such as HIV or hepatitis C who take care of themselves may actually live a long time.

2. Illegal Behaviors

There have been many reports in recent years concerning the influx of drug-related offenders in the prison system. The reports are accurate and reflect another common problem that people helping substance abusers will encounter. Since many of the substances being used are illegal, people are automatically criminalized by possessing the drugs they take. But the list of illegal behaviors also goes far beyond simple possession or even the sale of illegal substances. Instead, prisons are full due to a wide variety of drug-related infractions of varying severity, and a wide variety of people are in prison. Prisons are not full of dealers only.

It is impossible to predict who will turn to a religious community for assistance. I have counseled murderers, rapists, burglars, shoplifters, drunk drivers, male and female prostitutes, robbers and thieves, as well as those involved in dealing, all of whose criminal activities were associated in some way to drug and alcohol abuse. An effective ministry could counsel them all.

It is an important ministry that Christ has specifically commended to us, ministering to people who often elicit fear or anger from others, and whose experience of our culture is understandably punitive. They are people who victimize others and leave a great deal of harm in their wake. But attempting to help them is not as intimidating as it may sound. Unqualified acceptance, coupled with straightforward feedback, can accomplish a great deal.

One of my more interesting clients was a man in his late twenties who had just been released from prison. He first entered the penal system at the age of fourteen when he was sent into a youth detention facility for arson. Released two years later, he stabbed a man to death in a street fight and, at sixteen years old, found himself in state prison. He was referred to me by parole after doing twelve years.

The man had smoked marijuana during the few months in his teens that he was not behind bars, but refraining from drugs after his release did not seem to be difficult. A much greater problem during his transition to civilian life was holding a job. He had been imprisoned since the age of fourteen but now was mandated by parole to remain employed. He had never stayed employed before and found it hard. He was not used to the workday schedule, which was very different from the schedule he had during fourteen years in prison. He was exhausted. He had trouble taking orders from bosses, who threatened to report him to his parole officer. After one session, as he sat in my office in tears, I suggested he attend a welding school for vocational training, hoping that would give him a better chance to succeed. His parole officer approved. The last time I saw him, he was much happier and thankful for the advice.

Two days later, however, I read in the newspaper that he had helped beat a young man to death with a pistol. It was a vicious crime committed by a man who bore little resemblance to the person I had come to know. The person I knew was open about his struggles, grateful, and interested in finding his spirituality. I wondered if I had been conned, which is always a possibility. When he confessed to everything, I began to recognize him again; I had not been fooled. The reality of human behavior is much more complicated than either/or questions allow. I know he failed to tell me everything that was going on in his life and mind, but I also know he desired a straight life outside of prison walls. I had seen vulnerability in the character of this man who had twice committed murder, and whose unfortunate end was a life sentence.

Even the worst among us are human beings and can be known as such. Jeffrey Dahmer's father knew him as a son, not as a serial killer. There is much in the world that we will never understand. Nevertheless, we can still offer care, while we carefully maintain our boundaries.

For many who have been convicted of crimes, the underlying reason for the criminal activity was their efforts to subsidize their drug use. Drugs are expensive when used in substantial quantities every day. It is not unusual for people to spend an entire paycheck on crack during a weekend binge; when they become unemployed, of course, the pressure is even worse. The financial consultant, who was also a crack addict and alcoholic, described his money losses this way:

I lost a million dollars. I didn't smoke all of that, but I lost a million dollars. I probably smoked $200,000. I ran through it quick. . . . The consequences of what I did cost me a million dollars. Actually more than that. But, at the time, my balance sheet went from a million to a negative. . . . I went from having credit cards with about a hundred thousand dollar line to boosting stuff from a local store and returning it, in a matter of months.[3] It's a mistake to underestimate the power of a drug to an addict and what you'd be willing to do and sacrifice. . . . [Nonaddicts] cannot understand how somebody can do the things that they do, who wants this drug.

Many of the people arrested for selling drugs, for example, are street-level dealers looking to finance their own habits. The same need drives people who commit burglaries, who shoplift, and who engage in prostitution. They need quick cash. A prostitute can earn more money working the streets for a couple of hours than she could working a week in McDonalds. In addition, the money is tax free, and she will have a lot more free time for using drugs. Accomplished boosters support their drug use not only by stealing from stores and returning or reselling the wares, but also by taking special orders for particular makes of clothing or merchandise.

Sooner or later, they are caught and spend time in jail or

prison. But incarceration, on its own, rarely makes someone drastically change his or her manner of living. Most people vow never to return, after being released. I hear those words frequently in my work. As time passes, however, and the fear of prison eases, returning to the quick money is far too easy, especially when addiction is involved. Unless the addiction is successfully handled, prison is likely to become a part of the person's drug-use cycle.

For some, crime is an addiction in itself. For such people, life lived straight, within the law, is ultimately boring. There is excitement to life on the street, to the hustle, that becomes increasingly attractive as the routine of punching a clock for low wages becomes increasingly dreary. Add to that the large amounts of tax-free cash, cars, jewelry, and women that can come with the life, and the hold can be difficult to break. One recovering drug dealer discussed the criminal life this way:

TERRELL: I was so eager to [get into the business] because I wanted the big car, the women, the jewelry. You know, that's just part of that life.

CLINICIAN: There's a lot of money.

TERRELL: Oh yeah, a lot of money. A lot of money involved.

CLINICIAN: Tax free.

TERRELL: Yeah, tax free. Every dollar tax free.

CLINICIAN: Now you appreciate what that means, now that you're working.

TERRELL: Yeah. (Laughs) I wasn't getting a paycheck and saying, "What happened to all my money?"

CLINICIAN: It sometimes seems to me that [type of] life is just as addictive for some people as the drugs. They can't let go of it. And sometimes it's the money, but it's not always the money though.

TERRELL: Yeah. It's just a lifestyle. Women.

CLINICIAN: Right. The whole thing.

TERRELL: The whole thing. It's the whole thing. I found

one of the biggest things about that is being able to get what you want when you want it.

CLINICIAN: That can be nice. (Laughs)

TERRELL: Yeah. Being able to get what you want when you want it. That was one of the biggest things that I found out about [the life]. Because all the days that I was locked up, when I had to wait two weeks to spend $30, I'd say, "If I was on the streets hustling right now, I'd have so much s*** in my refrigerator I wouldn't know what to eat," you know? Or sitting there with the same pair of "Tims" [boots] for a year, that somebody thought about me and said, "OK, I'm gonna send him some boots." That's it though. Had them for a year. If I were on the streets hustling, I'd have a closet full of boots. I found that I missed getting what I want when I want it. Because we don't really travel. We don't really travel. We feel that if we travel we gonna miss something. You know. (Laughs) So it's not like we wake up one day and say, "OK, I'm gonna go to the Poconos," and just up and leave. "I'm gonna go to Florida." You find a lot of dealers, just like addicts, they stuck in the same place. The only place they know is them few blocks that all of this is goin on at. The only time they leave is when there's no more product and they have to go somewhere else to get it. And that's what, the next corner or probably the next house? A dealer says, "OK, I have no more product, and the price here is too high, so now I've got to go to the city." So what's that, three hours away? You still in New York. "Where you been?" "Oh, I just took a trip. Just went out of town." Out of town? (Laughs) You there and back before anybody know you gone. There's no traveling. I ain't been nowhere. Been doing this since I was eleven. And I traveled more, out of state, when I was young, before I started doing it, living with family, than I have since I've been hustling, since I been dealing.

CLINICIAN: It's very limiting in some ways.

TERRELL: Very limiting. Very limiting.

CLINICIAN: And after a while, the stuff gets boring, the jewelry and women and cars.

TERRELL: Yeah. It gets very boring. It gets very boring. And that's why you find a lot of . . . OK . . . "I got cars. I got jewelry. I got women. I need something. Something else. Something's missing." And that's when our drug of choice changes also. Because we're also looking for . . . OK . . . "This is not fun enough no more. Smoking weed, just partying, you know. So I know what I'll do. I'll sniff a little coke. Let me try this." You try it. You go to a party. Oh, the best party you ever been to! Now it's your drug of choice.

Criminality is another pattern of behavior that interferes with life and is not amenable to a person's efforts at self-control. People involved in criminal behaviors are not necessarily sociopathic; they are pulled back into a negative lifestyle by its apparent allure. The change to living life in a legitimate manner can be very difficult when temptation is so great.

3. Sexual Issues

There are a surprising number of ways that sexuality becomes enmeshed in substance abuse. The deleterious physical effects of drugs and the manner in which certain drugs stimulate the brain can lead alcohol and drug users into sexual problems that then become issues in their own right. Since sexuality is such a significant aspect of life, being aware of these difficulties is important.

One problem is dysfunction. Shakespeare put it like this, "[alcohol] provokes the desire but it takes away the performance" (*Macbeth*, act 2, scene 3). Since alcohol is a depressant, large amounts can interfere with physical arousal, causing impotence and retarded ejaculation in males and difficulty achieving orgasm in females. In the long-term, however, alcohol-damaged livers cause hormonal changes by enhancing the activity of liver enzymes that break down testosterone. This can produce a 50 percent decrease in the male hormone, leading to chronic impotence and infertility. Among women, damaged livers are unable to adequately turn estrogen into estradiol. This, in turn, interferes with vaginal lubrication and menstruation.

Drugs can also cause loss of interest in sex. People whose lifestyle is increasingly oriented around the use of a drug become less concerned about other aspects of their lives, including sex. If their addiction is highly developed and active, they may have no interest in sex at all, which then becomes a relationship problem. The impotence associated with drug use can contribute to this, as men avoid sex because they fear being unable to function and women avoid sex because they find it painful.

A different problem, primarily linked to cocaine and crack, is that a person's sexual urges and interests become exaggerated. Because cocaine stimulates the brain's "pleasure center," sexual desires can become inflated and extravagant. People find themselves indulging thoughts they might have otherwise dismissed. I have had clients who dressed in women's clothes or had homosexual relations only under the influence of cocaine. One young man confessed to me that he had lost his job due to a crack-induced compulsion to masturbate. He was away from his desk and in the men's room so frequently that he was fired.

An inflated sexuality can also lead people to engage in sexual binges in addition to crack binges. Perhaps hiring a prostitute, who may also supply the drugs, the addicted person spends days smoking crack and having sex in a compulsive manner. This often creates a forbidding cycle in which drug use and sex trigger and intensify each other. Whenever that person desires to have sex, he or she also desires to smoke crack, which creates an extremely potent relapse dynamic. In reverse, sex without cocaine seems boring and less intense. Recovery for cocaine addicts who have made this connection is much more difficult.

4. Family Problems

One of the most tragic results of addiction is the impact it can have on a family. It is not hard to imagine various kinds of family trauma when looking at what problems addiction can cause. It is unfortunate that unless addiction is successfully managed, that trauma will likely result in the dissolution of the family or the formation of damaging behavior patterns from which family members may never escape. It is in this situation that ministry to the addicted most readily moves beyond caring for the individual to caring for those with whom the substance abuser is involved. Religious communities in which families may already be engaged, and so have a basis of trust, are better situated than treatment agencies for providing extended care.

In my practice, I see a wide range of family trouble, some of which is extremely serious. While it is hard to say anything that negatively affects a family is not serious, some issues stand out as so grave as to merit immediate attention and intervention. These include domestic violence and neglected or abused children. Anyone working with addicts and their families is well advised to become acquainted with community resources, agencies that deal with these matters, and the reporting requirements.

Domestic violence is not unique to substance users, but it is often connected to substance abuse. People who have trouble handling their anger when straight and sober may find their rage breaking loose when using drugs; others, who do not normally exhibit an abusive temper, can become abusive. Alcohol and crack are the drugs most commonly connected to violent behavior, and the family is a common arena for that behavior to be enacted.

I have had many men tell me how much they loved the people they verbally, emotionally, sexually, or physically attacked, most often when they were drinking. Harold is a typical example. He married Gretchen six months earlier, and she was pregnant with their first child. They both appeared for his evaluation, which had been ordered by probation after his conviction for harassment. During a heated argument with his wife, her best friend had come to remove Gretchen from the house. Harold went outside, dented the friend's car, and spit in her face. The friend pressed charges. Of course, Harold was drunk.

Harold was not an imposing man, but when he was drinking, he routinely lost control and became a bully. During the evaluation, they openly discussed a time Harold had beaten Gretchen, three months into her pregnancy, sending her to the hospital. He did not get into trouble because she did not lose the baby, the hospital staff never asked about her injuries, and she was not about to tell. If Gretchen had lost the baby because of the beating, Harold could have faced manslaughter charges. Harold, again, was drunk and said he could not remember the incident because he had blacked out. But he did not doubt that he had inflicted the damage. Harold admitted that he became violent when he drank, while also professing a great love for his family.

The only response to this kind of irresponsible behavior is to expose the contradiction between Harold's words and his actions. Intervention is in order, coupled with a continual message that abuse can never be condoned or justified. When it comes to love, actions are most important. An appropriate first step is to admit the abuse of substances and people, followed by sincere efforts never to drink again. That would probably mean becoming actively engaged in counseling, joining a support group such as AA, and making friendships with other people who are recovering from alcoholism.

Several days later, Gretchen came to see me. Harold had continued to drink and was still verbally abusive. Since she had family in the area, I advised her to stay with her father until Harold quit using alcohol. If she had not had family nearby, I would have referred her to a shelter for abused women.[4] However, I was not surprised to receive a call from both partners two hours later; Gretchen had gone home, which is common conduct among people in abusive relationships. It is difficult for people to break out of their roles, whether they are victims or victimizers.

The other family issue requiring immediate intervention is child neglect or abuse. These are always the saddest cases.

People who are actively addicted and engaged in a binge cannot provide for their children and, at that moment, probably do not care. When their binges have ended, they may care very much, but that does not excuse the hours or days or weeks that their children were abandoned or given no attention or left to fend for themselves. In such situations, there is a legal and moral obligation to report the abuse. Parents can lose custody of their children.

Tyrone was a married father of three who worked full-time. He was sent for counseling by Child Protective Services after he had been reported for neglecting his children. His wife worked in the evenings, and he was responsible for watching the kids. One night, however, he wanted a six-pack of beer and left the children alone to go to the store. One of his children left the house and was found by police, wandering on the street. Unfortunately for Tyrone, despite saying all the right things in treatment and being closely watched by the authorities, he did exactly the same thing two more times. His wife left him so she would not lose the children, and Tyrone was prohibited from seeing his family for a year. He received a court order to complete counseling and abstain from alcohol.

Other problems that addictions cause in families are more mundane, but still problematic, and are often centered around the manner in which substance abusers are preoccupied with their drug of choice. They are less available for interaction, so relationships deteriorate. A great deal of money that the family needs is spent on alcohol or drugs. Living with such a person is like the proverbial problem of sleeping with an elephant, whether the person is an adult or child. The only way anybody gets rest is to kick the elephant out of bed. But that can be difficult to do. And if the family adjusts its behaviors to accommodate the user, thereby becoming more isolated as it guards the family secret, then they assume an addicted family identity.[5]

What is important to remember with these family issues is the necessity of first dealing with the substance abuse. Unless the family member quits using drugs, or is separated from the family unit, the family's other harmful dynamics will not change.

THE TWELVE STEP PROGRAM

The most effective program for dealing with addiction began as an unplanned meeting between two alcoholics. Bill W. was a chronic drinker who had failed numerous times to achieve sobriety. On a business trip to Akron, Ohio, in 1935, Bill found himself trying to resist his urge to drink and decided it might help to talk with someone else who knew exactly what he was going through. In the search for another alcoholic, he visited with Dr. Bob, whose own attempts to quit drinking had failed. Together, these two addicts found the sobriety that had eluded them and began to reach out for others as well.

As commonplace as self-help groups are today, they all trace their roots back to these two men. These groups are a twentieth-century phenomenon of tremendous importance, considering all the people who have been helped. Anyone working with the addicted needs to be acquainted with this group's methods. Alcoholics Anonymous and Narcotics Anonymous, specifically, remain excellent resources of help and are found in many communities across the country. Outside of AA and NA, there are extremely few places where addicts can meet openly with others like themselves and feel totally accepted.

The Twelve Steps, specifically, are based upon the experiences of the earliest AA members and summarize the process by which they achieved sober lives. They are steps that require action, based upon a simple premise. But they will have profound implications for anyone who works through them all.

The underlying principle for all Twelve Step groups is recognition of our human limitations. The First Step requires a person to admit his or her powerlessness when dealing with addiction. Being powerless is a special kind of problem, since it means a person lacks the ability, the willpower, the intelligence, or the strength to reach a solution on his or her own. In truth, powerlessness means hopelessness, unless those who are powerless receive help from something or someone stronger than themselves. Hope, then, is found, in the vocabulary of the Steps, in a higher power, or a source of strength outside of oneself, in which can be found the ability to do what cannot be done alone. Accepting one's need for a higher power is the purpose of Step Two and leads to the action of Step Three, in which a person turns his or her will and life over to the higher power, or God, as that person understands God.

Deep spirituality informs the Steps and is rooted in the beliefs of the program's founding members. While Bill W. had mixed feelings about organized religion, he believed in God; his final and successful attempt to become sober was initiated by a profound spiritual experience. Nevertheless, the concept of a higher power is left purposely vague and nondoctrinal to accommodate people of any belief within the recovery fellowship. Those who have difficulty believing in a God are encouraged to look at the group of fellow alcoholics as their higher power, thereby finding strength outside of themselves in the recovering community.

Beyond the belief in a higher power, spiritual principles inform each of the Steps.[6] There is an emphasis upon humility, surrender, honesty, reconciliation, and reaching out to others who are suffering. The Fourth, Fifth, Sixth, and Seventh Steps require a person to take an exhaustive moral inventory and then share with another human being the exact nature of his or her wrongs, with the goal of having God remove his or her character defects. The Eighth and Ninth Steps lead people to list all whom they have harmed and then make direct amends whenever possible, "except when to do so would injure them or others." The Tenth and Eleventh Steps seek the expansion of recovery by continuing the personal inventory, admitting wrongs on an ongoing basis, and deepening a conscious connection with God. The Twelfth Step has the recovering alcoholic reach out to others and seek to practice the steps in all of his or her affairs.[7]

It is important that these Steps have an order. For example, the personal inventory is meaningful only after a person has turned his or her will over to God, since only with God does a person have the ability to remove his or her character defects. Making amends is done only after taking the inventory, which makes clear how the addict has harmed people. Once all these actions have been accomplished, then they can be applied in a constant manner to all of life. Only at the end, after the previous Steps have been completed, is the recovering alcoholic led to reach out and be a mentor to others.

The original intention of the Twelve Step program was for the meetings and step work to be a joint process. A person in AA, for example, is advised to obtain a sponsor who has already done the work and can guide the newcomer through his or her own recovery. Like the manner in which Bill W. and Dr. Bob helped each other, sponsoring is based upon the idea that it takes an addict to know an addict. An addict will be able to empathize with struggles of another and to recognize an addict's manipulations and lies.

It is unfortunate that as Twelve Step programs have become more institutionalized, the discipline that characterized the original membership has diminished. Many people who attend meetings do not work the steps, and some attend meetings but do not have a real interest in becoming sober. There are continuing controversies, for example, over whether prison inmates or parolees should be mandated to attend Twelve Step meetings, since the meetings function well only for those who are motivated to get help. There are those who attend to socialize and those who look for dates (known as thirteenth stepping). Many have worked only the first three steps, since those are the ones usually covered in inpatient rehabilitation. Some make small amends but do not truly work through the process.

Similarly, many addicts resist going to meetings. They will complain that the fellowship is full of hypocrites or that the discussions are boring and people talk about the same thing repeatedly. They will say that meetings make them want to use drugs since drug use is discussed. They will say they do not go for any of that "higher power stuff." There are many parallels to the ways some people view church.

Nonetheless, drinkers and users who fully engage in a Twelve Step program will succeed in managing their addiction. As the AA book states, "Rarely have we seen a person fail who has thoroughly followed our path."[8] AA and NA fellowships remain a great resource for anyone wanting to help the addicted.

In order to encourage addicts to attend meetings, have a schedule of local meetings on hand to distribute.[9] The initial goal for the addict is to become at ease with the group. I recommend, in the beginning, supporting the idea of trying out different meetings. Not all AA or NA groups are the same. Some may attract a certain age group. Others, because of their location and time, may attract a professional crowd. The aim is to find a fellowship where a person is most comfortable and most likely to return. That meeting is a candidate for becoming a "home group," in which friendships are established and small responsibilities, like making the coffee, are accepted.

Meetings are a place to hear the stories of others and to discuss problems encountered in the struggle to become sober. Some meetings are open to the public; others are open only to alcoholics and addicts. Meeting schedules label the type of meetings being held. More than a place for talking, however, meetings are also a place to meet others in recovery, to build relationships, and to create a support network of like-minded people. Success depends upon the effectiveness of the connections an addict makes, including connections made beyond the larger group. Recovering friends, people to meet for coffee or to call when life gets tough, are essential. In fact, meeting for coffee makes it much more likely an addict will call those same people when a crisis occurs, and having a friend to call during a crisis is a key to staying sober.

The most personal relationship in the Twelve Step program is reserved for the sponsor. This is a one-on-one bond between one with substantial time in recovery and one who wants to learn the methods for achieving sobriety. The sponsor is a mentor, teacher, and coach and encourages and challenges the person desiring recovery to do what needs to be done. It is within this relationship that working through the Twelve Steps is most likely to occur.

SPIRITUALITY AND RECOVERY

Twelve Step fellowships refer to themselves as spiritual programs because of their emphasis upon receiving help from a higher power. This power is referred to as God, but the term has a proviso. God is whoever someone within the group believes God to be. As already discussed, the reason for the disclaimer is to prevent the program from excluding people by being doctrinally oriented or narrow. The defining element is not theological, but purposeful; the goal is to become well. Essential to that goal, however, is a belief in a power greater than oneself who can work effectively in the world, restoring people to sanity. This power provides direction to those willing to accept it and brings about a change of character that is otherwise impossible.

Considering how this program can work so well, while remaining theologically unsophisticated, merits some attention. For example, one of the results of the open-ended definition of God is that God means an astonishing variety of things. People in the "rooms," as meetings are commonly called, often refer to God as an anagram for "good orderly direction," with a vague notion that direction emanates from the group. I have counseled people who identified one of their children as being their higher power, denoting someone in whom they found positivity and motivation. Others have been taught their higher power can be a doorknob, as long as they focus upon the doorknob in a positive manner. Although I often attempt to help people find a more credible understanding of God, the efficacy of the program is not based upon how God is understood. Unlike so much religion, this form of spirituality is person-centered, not belief-centered.

Evaluated from that perspective, several features of the process stand out as linked to its effectiveness. One is the manner in which the self is moved. Rather than being the central focus of all attention, as self becomes for the addicted, that place is given to the God of their understanding.

While self-centeredness is a general human condition, addicts are remarkably selfish. As addiction progresses, obtaining and using drugs becomes all that matters, which also becomes a desire for instant gratification. Stephanie, the gambling addict, described her self-interest this way: "It's obsessive-compulsive behavior, an 'I don't care' attitude, the 'F' word, [with] no regard for others. I want what I want and I want it now. There is no higher good than what I need." The result was a religious family woman who stole from her employer and family.

Spirituality, by contrast, displaces the self from the center and replaces it with a higher power that is above any particular human want or concern. This new focus, if maintained, changes the way decisions are made and actions taken.

Ensuring that the self remains displaced, as recovery demands, requires activities that sustain this new context. These will be methods by which a person's chosen higher power is maintained in awareness and joined concretely to daily life. For example, if one wishes to use the fellowship of Alcoholics Anonymous as the higher power, then he or she will need to attend meetings, obtain a sponsor, and practice the Steps. These actions are not just good ideas; they are a means of connection from which context is created.

Because of the ubiquity of God in American culture, choosing God as a higher power can be problematic. Very frequently, clients will say they believe in God and rely upon God for help, when what they really believe in and rely upon is an idea. Without action, God is only an idea, and, as I repeatedly tell addicts, nice ideas will not keep you sober. The *idea* of God is a cultural artifact that lacks power.

Power is found in connection, and religious communities, by their nature, prescribe various methods by which connection with God is established. This may include worship, prayer, reading of scripture, and fellowship. People who choose God as their higher power will certainly have to join such a community.

One reason for this is the essential importance of being involved with other people, or a group, who share the same approach to God. The group provides a reservoir for friendships, as well as a forum for support and encouragement, where new behaviors are learned and integrity is monitored. Addicts are particularly adept at discerning and confronting the lies and manipulations of other addicts. For example, I had a client who identified himself as a Pentecostal Christian, but he spoke in tongues primarily when he was drunk. He predictably was not involved in a church where he divulged his manner of expressing the Spirit.

Not oriented around beliefs, this form of spirituality is based upon action and relationships. Ideas are not the currency of exchange. Behavior and connection are what count.

And these actions, maintained within the relationships of a supportive fellowship, result in a discipline. New forms of conduct promote and enforce each other, when linked within an overall behavioral structure. Whereas attendance at meetings or worship and the submission of the self might be difficult initially, with practice and involvement they become the norm. This redefinition of normalcy is how lifestyles change and long-term recovery is possible.

From this point of view, addictions can be understood as ruling patterns of behavior, as disciplines oriented around the self, which can be altered only by a change of context. Such self-centered disciplines thrive in a culture that reveres the self and that maintains what the early sociologist Emile Durkheim referred to as the cult of the individual. He believed this cult was a natural outgrowth of modernism and, along with its attendant values, was destined to replace traditional religion in modern societies. Social forces would elevate the individual, with individual rights and individual achievement, to the highest good.

In such a situation, whatever helps generate individual success and productivity is valued and results in a profoundly ironic cultural reality: Behaviors that go to the core of addiction are socially esteemed in other contexts. This state of affairs leads to the further conclusion that addiction is encouraged and fostered by particular aspects of modern culture. The financial consultant, who was also an alcoholic and crack addict, saw it this way:

DONALD: [Our culture rewards people who] are excessive. Absolutely. I mean, we don't find anyone who has grown up to achieve what we hold up to be the epitome of success in our society, who has balance.

CLINICIAN: You don't become President by having balance.

DONALD: You don't become Michael Jordan by having balance. You don't become Tiger Woods by having balance. And I'm not making character assessments of these people. But I don't need to know them to know that they were willing to do things that other people weren't willing to do to get where they went. Now that can have positive benefits, but there's always a cost: to their family, to [themselves].

CLINICIAN: So the irony is that while we live in a culture [that] encourages excess, people are still mystified and clueless when it comes to addiction.

DONALD: True, but the values of overachievement and money and workaholism and obsessiveness—those are things that are rewarded in our society. Smoking crack isn't.

CLINICIAN: So they can look at you and say, "How come you're so dishonest and so manipulative?"

DONALD: When they did the same thing the day before, . . . screwing somebody in a real estate deal.

CLINICIAN: You were lying about a drug instead of lying about making money, and that they don't get.

DONALD: Absolutely.

In this type of cultural climate, spirituality means anything that can carry a person beyond himself or herself, which redresses the imbalances associated with the cult of individuality. A program that displaces the self, underscores its limits, emphasizes relationships, and surrounds people with a human fellowship of equalizing acceptance is found to be healing. Twelve Step programs, specifically, are deeply and subtly countercultural.

Churches that minister effectively to addicts will find themselves cultivating their own roots. These roots, which predate the modern era, have placed religious communities at odds with much within modern culture, and the success of Twelve Step programs demonstrates that this incompatibility need not mean failure. But the conflict needs to be engaged at the level of the person, rather than on ideology. The compelling issue is not science versus religion or liberal morality versus traditional beliefs. It is the intense human necessity to deal with limitation and find connections beyond the self. That is the lesson the addicted have to teach us.

---

1. James C. McKinley Jr., "Strawberry Says His Colon Cancer Has Returned," *New York Times* (29 July 2000), D1.

2. Darryl Inaba and William Cohen, *Uppers, Downers, All Arounders: Physical and Mental Effects of Psychoactive Drugs*, 2nd ed. (Ashland, Ore.: CNS Productions, 1993), 256.

3. "Boosting" is street jargon for shoplifting.

4. It is a good idea to be aware of the location of the nearest shelter and how to refer people.

5. An excellent book on this topic is *The Alcoholic Family* by Peter Steinglass (New York: Basic Books, 1987).

6. Books fully explaining the Twelve Steps can be found in any well-stocked bookstore.

7. *Alcoholics Anonymous: The Story of How Many Thousands of Men and Women Have Recovered from Alcoholism,* 3rd ed. (New York: Alcoholics Anonymous World Services, 1976), 59-60.

8. Ibid., 58.

9. Schedules can be picked up at meetings. Feel free to attend an open meeting for your own information.

3

Methods for Ministry

Derrick has walked in your office. He is a parishioner in his early thirties, with a wife and young son and has been coming to church about three years. An accountant by profession, Derrick has recently joined the Finance Committee and volunteered to help audit the church's books at the end of the year. Still, you do not know him very well. You have had only casual conversations together. Several weeks ago, however, he did mention that he would like to talk, and you set up a time to get together.

He appears slightly uncomfortable as he sits down and engages in a little small talk. But after a few minutes, Derrick says he has a problem to discuss and gives you a brief personal history. He did not get married until he was twenty-seven. He had enjoyed his single life and the freedom to do as he pleased. He went out often, liked to party, and drinking was part of the lifestyle. Drinking had never been a problem. But now, his wife is giving him a hard time about his use of alcohol.

She did not seem to mind before the baby was born last year, but lately she has complained quite a bit. They have had some heated arguments about it. Then, last week, she accused him of driving drunk and said she had had enough. She was worried that he was going to cause a wreck. She was worried about the example he would set for their child. She wanted him to get some help. Since Derrick really did not want to talk to any alcohol counselors, he agreed that he would talk to you.

Why Derrick chose you and the real source of the trouble he is describing is not clear at this point. He may have come to you because he is a religious man or because you appear to offer a sympathetic ear, but he may also be hoping you are less knowledgeable than an alcohol counselor. His motives, as well as the nature of his problem, will become apparent only after evaluating his situation.

ASSESSMENT

When someone like Derrick asks for help, the source of his trouble will not necessarily be obvious. For example, it is possible that his drinking patterns are socially acceptable, while not acceptable to his wife. In that case, unless he is willing to accede to his wife's wishes, marital counseling would be the appropriate course of action. But it is also true that if Derrick does have an unacknowledged drinking problem, he will believe his interests are best served by making the difficulty appear to be a relational one. Until an addict is ready to quit, concealment, deception, and deflection are always the first stratagems.

Those ploys place caregivers in the position of detectives, of sorts, attempting to discern the disposition of a problem from someone who may not be wholly open or honest. With any potential substance abuser, the level of honesty offered must be determined, along with the patterns of drug use, by eliciting the user's story, listening carefully, and looking for the symptoms already discussed.

A clinician would subject Derrick to a formal evaluation, asking questions in order to complete a pre-established questionnaire. Such a questionnaire covers a variety of topics, including: alcohol and drug use history, a personal history, legal involvements, medical issues, mental health concerns, and employment status. As each topic is covered, a clinician attempts to ascertain the veracity of the parts by cross-referencing them with one another. Oftentimes, one part of the story is belied by other aspects of a person's history.

Not being a clinician, a pastor who is knowledgeable about substance abuse is freer to search for the same information in a more personal manner. Assuming a conversational approach, instead of a structured diagnostic interview, a pastor can begin simply by asking Derrick to tell more about himself. Where did he grow up? Are his parents still alive? How long has he been married? Has he been married before? Where does he work? How long has he been at that job? What does he do for fun? By starting with nonthreatening questions in a relaxed manner, the pastor can sketch a picture of who he is as a person; but even these questions, while far from intimidating, can highlight the possible problems. If he was previously married, what caused the divorce? Perhaps alcohol was an issue. If he is unemployed or has had numerous jobs, drug abuse can be a reason. If he does not do much in the way of fun, maybe it's because he spends a lot of time drinking. Or is drinking always included in his idea of fun?

After establishing a more personalized rapport, it is easier to approach the issue of alcohol and drug use. Even people whose use of alcohol is nonabusive can easily become defensive, and, very commonly, that defensiveness results in underreporting the frequency of their drinking or the amounts they consume. This more likely will be the case when they are talking with someone regarded as a moral authority, and escalate even higher if the drugs being used are illegal. Accordingly, talking about other issues first can make a person feel safer, while also providing a context in which to view his or her drug use.

A good way to open the issue of alcohol use is by asking in a straightforward manner when Derrick last had a drink. Placing that question up front is more likely to get an honest response, especially if Derrick begins to feel self-protective. How often does he drink and how much? How old was he when he first began drinking? Has he ever tried to quit before or had alcohol counseling? The goal is to gain a picture of his drinking habits, since Derrick has identified alcohol as the primary drug in question. However, we always inquire about other drugs. Has he ever used anything else? Has he ever smoked marijuana, sniffed cocaine, or taken acid? We never assume by appearances what someone might do. He may say he last used pot when he was a teen, or he may admit to smoking an occasional joint with friends. If he does disclose any current use of other drugs, then we gain a fuller picture of that use as well.

Since Derrick mentioned that his wife accused him of driving while intoxicated, that would be an incident to explore more fully. Where had he been? How much did he drink? Why did she think he was drunk? Has he ever had a DWI? Derrick had also mentioned his lifestyle before he was married. What were his drinking habits then? How have they clashed with his new married lifestyle?

Once we begin to explore his use of alcohol and drugs, we should not be afraid to ask whatever we need to know. Many times people are anxious to talk, especially if they know or suspect there is a problem; they are simply looking for a safe place and someone who shows an interest. We can inquire about any medical, mental health, or legal issues, since they are often related to substance abuse. After a knowledgeable and focused conversation, we will gain a much clearer picture of the problems Derrick is facing. Below is a list of basic issues that can help to assess someone for possible substance abuse.

Personal	Substance Use	Related Issues
Age	Last use	Medical health
Marital history	How often/how much	Mental health
Education level	Age when started	Legal problems
Employment	Previous attempts to quit	
Hobbies/Fun	Previous counseling	
	Other drugs	

The importance of confidentiality must be stated from the beginning. As a basis for encouraging honesty, confidentiality is essential, even when we know information that we wish others knew. Within clinical and medical agencies, it is against the law to reveal personal information without written permission. This law can be broken only if a clinician believes a crime is going to be committed, a person is imminently suicidal, or a signed court order is served.

Pastors have more legal latitude and, as a result, need to decide the extent of the confidentiality they will offer. Will there be limits to the information we are willing to keep to ourselves? In making that decision, however, keep in mind the church's tradition of privileged communication. The inviolability of the priestly confessional is a good example. Rooted in the biblical notion of sanctuary, that privilege is accorded recognition by our society.

Although the maintenance of confidentiality can lead to personal discomfort, at times, the clinical guidelines are a useful measure. If Derrick, unbeknownst to his wife, has begun to smoke crack and utilize prostitutes or even reveals that he has a sexually transmitted disease, that may not be knowledge we unilaterally share with his wife or anyone else. When dealing with substance abuse, such situations may well occur and make knowing how much Derrick has revealed to others very important. Although Derrick can be encouraged to become more honest, his secrets will be our own.

The goal of any assessment, of course, is to determine if the use of alcohol or other drugs shows a pattern of interfering in a person's life. That is the meaning of abuse and is sufficient to warrant an intervention. Since any pattern of interference will have demonstrable, negative consequences, making those consequences clear is where intervention will begin. What may not be immediately apparent is whether any maladaptive patterns of behavior are subject to a person's efforts at self-control. That determination can wait, however. We are looking for people for whom drinking alcohol or using drugs causes recurring problems. Such people need not be addicted to also require help.

If Derrick is having some kind of repeated problem associated with his drinking, an effective evaluation will identify its nature. The *DSM-IV* criteria are most useful as a list of common ways that substance use interferes with life: tolerance, withdrawal, exceeding intentions, failed attempts to quit, poor use of time, interfering with important roles and activities, making problems worse. Discerning whether someone abuses substances will then help determine the best ways to offer ministry.

REFERRAL

When talking with Derrick, suppose that he claims the last time he drank alcohol was last night. He drinks a beer or has a cocktail three or four times a week after coming home from the office. He does not see that as a big deal. His wife occasionally complains about his breath when he drinks, but what most irritates her is his habit of meeting friends on Sunday afternoon to watch a ballgame, play some cards, and drink beer. He began this routine before he was married and would like to carry it on. However, since the baby was born, his wife has been very vocal about her annoyance. She does not like being left home while he is out drinking with friends. She thinks Sunday should be a family day. Now that they have a child, she wants him to quit partying.

There was a time when they would go dancing and both have a few drinks, but that time has ended. His wife stopped drinking all alcohol when she became pregnant and does not understand why he needs to continue. The problem came to a head two weeks ago when his car slid off an icy road while he was driving home from his Sunday get-together. His wife accused him of driving under the influence; he said he drank only four beers. That is when he agreed to talk to you. He denies using any other drugs since he was a teenager and has never had counseling for substance abuse.

In this scenario, Derrick qualifies as a moderate drinker. Although he drinks alcohol four to five days a week, the amount he consumes is not large, at least not compared to a heavy drinker who might imbibe three or four six-packs in an evening. Accordingly, he probably has not developed a high tolerance, nor will he manifest severe withdrawal symptoms the next day. If we take his story at face value, Derrick's drinking did not interfere with any part of his life until his wife changed her lifestyle after becoming pregnant. Now it is part of a relational conflict. As for the accident, even if Derrick drank more beer than he admitted, he does not show a pattern of impaired driving. That would change, however, with a second, similar incident.

A logical follow-up to this assessment of the problem is to suggest a joint counseling session with Derrick and his wife. Because the trouble appears at the outset to be interpersonal, rather than one of abusing substances, talking with both people together is a reasonable proposal and also provides the opportunity to check Derrick's description of his alcohol use against that of his wife. Assuming that Derrick's reporting is accurate, marital counseling for their differing values would be a suitable course of action.

This would change entirely if Derrick admits to secretly smoking an occasional joint at his Sunday afternoon sessions with friends. He does not buy it or bring it, but he partakes. Important is that his wife does not suspect him of using drugs, and he is not about to tell her, because he knows she would be very upset. Technically, his use of an illegal substance qualifies as abuse since he is putting himself in legal jeopardy. But, more significant, the dishonesty caused by his drug use is interfering with his role as a husband; accepting that dishonesty in a marriage is a breach of trust. As Derrick's mendacity indicates, his desire to get high routinely overrides his better judgment and his fear of the consequences. In this case, substance abuse counseling would be in order, as his use of a drug is the underlying cause of his problem.

Let's suppose a different scenario. Derrick claims the last time he drank alcohol was last night. When he gets home after work, he makes himself a drink or two. He does not see that as a big deal; it is just part of the world he moves in. Quite commonly, for example, he has a couple of cocktails when he meets clients for lunch; that is part of the cost of business and schmoozing his customers. He is never drunk, he says, and he has learned to schedule a light workload after these business lunches. On Fridays, he has a standing golf engagement with a couple of friends. Yes, they bring a cooler of beer in the golf cart, but the whole point is to unwind at the end of the week. They stop at the Nineteenth Hole when they have finished their game; the high scorer buys a round or two, and Derrick heads home.

When asked if he drinks every day, Derrick agrees but insists that he does not have a problem. The one with the problem, he believes, is his wife. She refuses to leave him alone with the baby in the evening because she thinks he drinks too much. He tried not drinking on some days, so that his wife could get out and run some errands, but it was too much of a hassle. Instead, he challenged her to point out one time he appeared drunk, which she could not do. Her only response was that he gets belligerent when he drinks. Getting pulled over by a cop on the way home from the golf club just added fuel to the fire, even though charges were never filed. He works hard. He brings home good money. If alcohol helps him relax, what is it to her? he thinks. She used to drink, too. Nevertheless, she is being extremely difficult and has even threatened to leave if he does not get help. Derrick is hoping you can help his wife become more reasonable.

Unfortunate for Derrick, he is showing some symptoms. We would expect someone who drinks a couple of alcoholic beverages every day to have developed some tolerance, which is supported by his claim never to feel drunk. A light drinker would most likely feel tipsy or intoxicated consuming the same amount as Derrick. Even his claim not to be drunk, though, is partially contradicted by his reduced workload after his business lunches. He apparently feels less able to work effectively and is allowing alcohol to interfere with his job. He is also allowing alcohol to interfere with his role as a parent. Knowing that his wife will not leave him alone with his son, Derrick continues to drink on the days he could tend his child. He tried to abstain on those times, found himself unable to follow through for more than a week or two, and eventually quit trying. It may be that Derrick is unable to quit. In that case, Derrick is not merely abusing alcohol; he is addicted to it. Without help, his alcoholism will probably drive away his family, and who knows what else down the road.

Under these circumstances, helping Derrick become involved in substance abuse counseling is the appropriate action. We need to be acquainted with the local agencies and offer to make a personal referral. It is a good idea to introduce Derrick to someone in AA, if Derrick is willing. But, above all, we should expect him to be resistant. Helping a substance abuser overcome his or her recalcitrance is how treatment starts and, if successful, is a significant achievement.

INDIVIDUAL COUNSELING

There are two essential ways that a pastor or caregiver from a religious community can offer vital individual ministry to substance abusers or addicts. One, just mentioned, is by identifying people who have drug abuse problems and persuading them to get help. The other is by giving ongoing support to a person's efforts at recovery. The challenge and importance of these two roles cannot be overstated.

When Derrick was in your office, he was not necessarily interested in looking at himself. He was probably hoping to mollify his wife and maybe enlist you in the cause. Talking to him, however, has revealed a different problem that Derrick is ignoring or to which he is blind. Helping Derrick see his drug abuse must occur before he will change and before his family will find some peace.

Accomplishing that goal is not an easy task. Many forces work together to create addictive behavior patterns, which are often self-reinforcing and beyond anyone's control. Similarly, pastors do not have the authority of a judge to order people to get counseling and quit using drugs and to threaten them with jail if they do not comply. A pastor's authority and power, by contrast, rests in relationships—with Derrick and with the One who created him. You work with him but do not rush him. Remember the importance of patience, honesty, and withholding judgment. You are ready to suggest meeting together again. And you pray with him.

The basic message needs to center on the negatives that drug use is introducing into his life. These negatives, after all, are the only reason to quit. Using the examples he has given, we show specifically how alcohol or drugs are interfering with his life and causing damage. In Derrick's case, his marriage is deteriorating. He could lose his family. He becomes argumentative. His wife does not find him trustworthy. He accomplishes less at work. He has tried to abstain and failed. With Derrick's permission, his wife can be invited to a session to express her feelings. How can Derrick be helped to see himself?

Even then, success may not happen. You assure him that the office door is open and pray that a seed of recovery was planted.

If Derrick is willing to get help, or at least to see how counseling feels, you would recommend referring him to a professional agency that deals with substance abuse. One reason is that agencies will do drug testing, and testing can be an extremely useful tool in the attempt to keep addicts honest.[1] More important, you will then be free to function as a support person outside of treatment.

As someone who works professionally in the field, dealing every day with people who abuse drugs of all kinds, I cannot overemphasize the value of that supportive role. Unlike psychotherapy, which tends to be a more solitary exploration of the psyche, recovery from substance abuse must take place in the community, on the streets. The addict must learn ways to deal with a culture that subtly encourages addiction, as well as with the ubiquitous availability of drugs, and that cannot be done in the confines of an office. As a result, counseling primarily involves helping people establish a support network outside of treatment, which they can utilize the rest of their lives, rather than rely on therapists. However, outside of Twelve Step programs, there is a dearth of places to find that support. Churches and clergy can provide a tremendous resource that can have a deep and lifelong impact upon people struggling with drug abuse.

Support, in this sense, is not complicated. It requires maintaining an active relationship with those attempting recovery, reinforcing the basic methods used for successful recovery, offering encouragement, as well as conveying a challenge to continued growth. This can and should include spiritual input. Meeting together for coffee once or twice a month, having a prayer, being available to call if a crisis hits or a person is dealing with an urge to get high, will be a great help to a recovering addict. In return, we will get to know people for whom we can develop tremendous respect.

RECOVERY BASICS

There are a few basic techniques everyone attempting to recover from addiction needs to practice. Preparing someone for referral, functioning in a supportive role, and offering individual counseling are essential methods to help the addicted implement these techniques in their lives. Most of the time, relapse occurs because one of these simple actions was neglected.

1. The first rule of recovery is to "avoid people, places, and things." This is shorthand for avoiding people who use drugs, places where drugs are used or sold, and paraphernalia that accompanies drug usage. One of the biggest problems for those new in recovery, for example, is handling their friends who still use drugs or drink. If they continue to hang around while their friends smoke a blunt or crack or pop open a beer, chances are nearly 100 percent that eventually those individuals will fall back into using drugs. No matter how motivated they may be, a day will come when they get high with their friends because, for whatever reason, they simply did not care that day.

The same is true about places. An alcoholic cannot spend much time sitting at the bar without ultimately resuming his drinking habits. He may order a soft drink the first five times he sits on the stool, but he will end up drunk sooner or later. In the same manner, a pot smoker cannot stash her favorite bong and still quit smoking marijuana for the long-term. Failure to get rid of smoking devices is actually a reservation about quitting in the first place.

2. Rule number two of recovery is to abstain from all mood-altering drugs. Most substance abusers are able to identify a drug of choice, meaning the drug they most desire. Oftentimes, they will try to avoid using that particular drug, while continuing to use others. For example, crack addicts will frequently smoke pot in lieu of crack, attempting to employ a "marijuana maintenance program." They will justify the substitution with several rationalizations: Marijuana is much less harmful than crack, is not their drug of choice, and helps them avoid crack. But it does not work. People who substitute one drug for another usually end up returning to the drug they most crave.

An example is Jamaal, a client on felony probation for stealing money from his employer to buy crack. Being on felony probation meant that he had been given a break by not having to go to state prison. He did several months in the county jail, instead, and met with a probation officer after his release, which was a lenient sentence. If he violated the rules of his probation, however, state prison would be his destination.

Jamaal had every intention of never smoking crack again. He had a wife and a home. He had the skills to find decent jobs. He knew he was lucky not to be "doing state time." But he liked to drink and liked to justify his drinking by arguing that alcohol was legal. His problem with drinking, though, was that when he drank a certain amount, he would lose control, and smoking crack was one of the results. Alcohol lowered his inhibitions and diminished his capacity to think clearly, so he made poor decisions. Nevertheless, he refused to quit. Within six months, after a night of drinking, he bought crack at a spot where the police watched constantly. He was arrested, his probation was revoked, and he was sent to state prison for two years.

Using no drugs has to be the unvarying message. When an addict begins to justify drug use of any kind, his or her excuses need to be challenged and total abstinence held as an unequivocal standard. Doors that are not locked will eventually be opened.

3. Rule number three is that few recover alone. Addicts who fail in recovery usually do so because they did not get help or stopped utilizing the help they had begun. Being on their own, they are overwhelmed by their cravings, by their problems, and by their emotions, and pick up drugs again.

There is often a negative image attached to the idea of getting help, which is why some people will drive around lost for hours before requesting directions. But pride will kill an addict. We impress upon people with whom we talk the fact that successful people rarely attain their achievements totally on their own. Rather, most successful people are adept at finding good people to help them. Michael Jordan was the best basketball player of his generation, yet he learned that he could not win alone. He involved his teammates and recognized the importance of his coach. It is a message that addicts must learn also.

Twelve Step programs are an obvious and immediate place for anyone who abuses substances to seek help. Even at these meetings, however, one must seek help from those who are succeeding themselves. That is especially true when selecting someone to serve as a sponsor or mentor. Hopefully churches, including the readers', will also become known as fellowships where effective help can be found for addicts.

4. *Recovery rule number four is to deal openly with emotions.* One of the hardest aspects of achieving long-term recovery (meaning abstinence for more than a year) is learning to identify feelings and handling them appropriately. All substance abusers, to varying degrees, use drugs as a way to handle uncomfortable feelings. While that is never the only reason someone takes drugs, it becomes one of the ongoing motivations. If we are sad, angry, anxious, scared, frustrated, or lonely, there is a way to relieve those symptoms with almost instantaneous results. One disadvantage of that strategy, however, is that addicts forget how to distinguish and express their emotions, if they ever knew in the first place. They tend to be emotionally arrested at the age they began serious drug use. That, in itself, explains a lot of behaviors observed on the streets.

If we were to ask an addict to specify what he or she is feeling, likely responses would be "I don't feel good" or "I feel OK." When asked to be specific, they often cannot because they are trying to handle a conglomerate of vague emotions. They do not know how to identify needs and feelings. To sustain their recovery, addicts must become more skilled at discriminating those emotions so they can constructively handle them.

Recognizing feelings is not an easy task, but the way to begin is by talking to others about those feelings. Providing a list of basic emotions from which people can pick, in order to name their moods and identify feelings, is a simple but effective tool.

In that manner, with feedback, they become more adept at recognizing what they are feeling. At the same time, they are practicing a valuable method for processing those feelings, without getting high. Learning to talk effectively about emotions can be difficult for many people, not just for addicts, but for addicts it is a foundation for sobriety. Relapses are often caused by emotions that are not handled openly and prudently.

5. *A final rule for successful recovery is to maintain a positive attitude.* Negativity, hopelessness, frustration, impatience, arrogance, self-dislike, and ingratitude are all mental positions that easily lead to drug use by encouraging a sense of "what does it matter?" Nevertheless, avoiding negativity can be tricky, especially when addiction has probably left its victims in tough circumstances and surrounded by people with the same attitudes.

Part of staying positive is retaining a sense of humility. Remembering that everyone has limitations and flaws, maintaining realistic expectations, and remaining open to help are remedies for the impatience and arrogance that afflict addicts. However, because of natural defensiveness, guarding against the pain caused by guilt and shame, those are not necessarily easy positions to retain.

In response, as a way of defusing that defensive posture, addicts need encouragement to recognize their blunders and defects without the accompanying shame. The church, in particular, is often regarded by many addicts as a shame-inducing institution. But Jesus never said, "Blessed are the guilty." Guilt and shame are not effective motivators to change; rather, they become part of a behavioral pattern in which nothing ever changes.

Humility is also made difficult to obtain by false ideas about our own importance. Drug users, specifically, may struggle with self-importance, not because of their great achievements, but because drug use fuels fantasies of achievement, particularly among those who smoke marijuana chronically. Pot-heads regard themselves as better than other addicts, by and large, because they often have inflated self-images supported by marijuana use. It is not unusual, for example, for heavy marijuana smokers to think they are remarkably deep thinkers. But illusory beliefs eventually result in negativity and need to be challenged with reality.

A related key for keeping a positive attitude is maintaining a sense of gratitude. Being able to give thanks for even the small things—for the incremental steps of progress and small victories in recovery—can affect a person's entire demeanor. It is insurance against a life spent in complaint. Addicts do well to keep in mind the definition of pessimism and optimism. A pessimist is a child in a room full of toys, complaining that there's nothing to play with. An optimist is a child in a room full of horse manure, digging gleefully because he or she is sure there's a pony in there somewhere. That kind of optimism is necessary to succeed in recovery.

In working with the addicted, these basic methods for successful recovery should inform the relationship. People who practice them consistently will achieve long lasting change.

FAMILY COUNSELING

A similar strategy is employed when dealing with the family members of someone who abuses drugs. As already discussed, an active alcoholic or drug addict quickly creates a toxic situation that poisons all relationships in which he or she is involved. This is not just because drug users are mostly emotionally unavailable, but also because of their anger, their dishonesty, their stealing, and the embarrassment they cause. Until the drug use stops, or the user is removed, the associated people cannot begin to heal.

Accomplishing either of those goals, however, can be extremely difficult. All family members or friends can do, if they are willing to deal with the situation, is manage their own relationships with the user, who is a master at manipulating those same relationships. This means that family members and friends must prepare before taking any interventive or remedial action and will require a lot of support.

Andrea and Bill had adopted a ten-year-old boy when they were in their early forties. Andrea was a teacher, and Bill was a deputy in the sheriff's office. Scott, whose biological parents had been drug addicted and neglectful, quickly became the center of their lives. Scott had problems through his school years, but nothing serious resulted from them, partly because of his parent's connections, and partly because of his own personal charm. Extremely good-looking, Scott had learned how to use his looks to his advantage. Real trouble did not arise until after he graduated from high school.

After high school, Scott found a job as a security officer but also began to party a lot. Although he had smoked weed before, he was now smoking every day. He would strap a vial of clean urine to his leg so that he could pass the random drug screens conducted at his job. He still lived at home. Although he had agreed to pay rent, he frequently claimed to have no money. His parents lent him the funds to buy a Camaro, but he was defaulting on that obligation, too. If his mother nagged him about making payments, he would become verbally abusive, sometimes threaten her physically, and then move in with one of his many girlfriends. Eventually, however, Scott would return home and sweet-talk his way in the door, only to begin the cycle again. This continued until his parents finally had him arrested on harassment charges. He was placed on probation and sent to treatment.

In our counseling sessions, Scott revealed that one of the reasons he did not pay his parents the money he owed was that he was spending so much on marijuana, as well as on drinking in clubs. He felt they owed him a place to stay. He resented having been adopted in the first place, and his anger led to a sense of entitlement. When he lost his job for failing to show up, it did not affect his style very much. He did not have any bills, and if his mother did not give him money, he would take some.

Like most people who are addicted to marijuana, Scott lacked motivation to change or to accomplish much with his life. When high on marijuana, users care very little, which is one reason they like to smoke. When not using, they may tell themselves they are going to accomplish this or that, but, as soon as they get high again, their ambitions disappear. That is why Scott did not mind living with his parents in his twenties. Because he was addicted, all that really mattered to him was himself and his ability to keep himself supplied. Many chronic pot users, like Scott, also show an increased irritability and restlessness when not smoking, which exacerbated the anger he already felt about being abandoned by his biological parents.

I wish I could say treatment ended with positive results. Instead, Scott never quit smoking pot, even with probation on his back. His mother was receiving counseling from another clinician, in an effort to set stronger boundaries, but the father never attended. When joint sessions for the mother and son were scheduled, she was the one who repeatedly did not show up. Once they finally did meet together, Scott announced that he was going to do whatever he wanted and verbally intimidated his mother. Fearing for everyone's safety, we asked him to leave the building and called the police when he refused.

I also wish I could say Scott's case was unusual. Rather, he's a good example of how an addict can toxify a family and challenge the character flaws of everyone involved, further impairing their ability to handle a very difficult problem. That is why family members or friends who decide to intervene—and many never make that effort—must prepare themselves emotionally and have a clear plan. Otherwise, their efforts will probably fail.

When a family member approaches you, there are several ways to provide concrete help. One is to listen to the story. If, indeed, that person is dealing with an addict within the family structure, you will need to provide reassurance that the one seeking the help is not the crazy one. Deflecting responsibility and attempting to convince family members that others are the ones at fault is a common and effective tactic for people attempting to hide their defects.

Second, strongly encourage the family members to attend Al-Anon or a similar self-help program. Al-Anon is based on the Twelve Steps and is specifically for those whose friends or family abuse substances. People who have been in similar circumstances are effective resources for learning how to handle an addict in the family and can provide practical advice. Addicts often openly admit that their schemes no longer work well when their spouses or partners become involved in Al-Anon meetings.

Referring family members for counseling at a substance abuse agency is also a good idea. Agencies offer help to families of addicts, assisting them in establishing firmer boundaries, deciding upon a plan of action, and involving the members in joint counseling, as was attempted with Scott and his mother. Generally, joint sessions attempt to raise the awareness of the substance user in regard to his or her own behaviors, especially as experienced by that person's significant others, and to make contracts for changing those behaviors. It is important that contracts have unambiguous goals and consequences.

Above all else, maintain contact and provide support personally, regardless of the choices family members make. Family members cannot be forced to intervene, but continuing to provide affirmation may help them take action later. If they do, the backing and encouragement of others who are knowledgeable will be absolutely necessary because of the addict's resistance and the difficult choices that may have to be made.

This support will be especially needed if circumstances lead to the eviction of a family member who refuses to abstain or alter his or her behaviors. Although that may be required for a family to regain its health, and may be one of the consequences of a contract enacted by the family during the course of counseling, few decisions are more difficult to carry out. Forcing a recalcitrant, addicted member to leave the home is emotionally wrenching, and people will need help dealing with their guilt, self-doubts, and fears for their loved one.

When family members face traumatic choices, it is especially important to maintain our boundaries carefully. People making apparently poor decisions or choosing to remain in dysfunctional settings can stimulate the "rescuer" in us all. But pushing people to take action for which they are not prepared will create additional problems.

I am reminded of a story about the psychotherapist Otto Rank. A woman came to him for consultation after suffering from periodic attacks of intestinal trouble, which her doctors had been unable to remedy. She had concluded that her indigestion was an emotional problem, a deduction with which Rank agreed; nevertheless, he chose not to engage her in therapy. He was not convinced that she was ready or able to address whatever deeper issues might be uncovered: "It is not so much a question as to whether we are able to cure a patient, whether we can or not, but whether we should or not."[2] In making the decision to treat a person, the goal should be what is best for the patient and his or her family, and the impetus for action must always come from the person seeking help.

GROUPS

It seems clear that a primary provision Jesus made for continuing his mission after his death was establishing a select group. Whatever may have been the composition and structure of that original bunch, Jesus did not intend for Christianity to be a solitary experience. There is strength in a group that arises from feelings of solidarity, from its shared collective wisdom, and from the ability of members to hold one another accountable. We read about Paul confronting Peter, in that spirit, in Galatians 2:11.

This group experience has been diminished somewhat for the Christian community by the numbers of people involved and the routines of modern culture. It is difficult to hold one another accountable when we do not know one another's name, let alone what is going on in other people's lives. A traditional sense of community is waning as people are increasingly mobile and connected globally, because these changes also lead, ironically, to more isolated lives. The term "global community" is an oxymoron.

That addiction is, as we know it, a modern development, is no accident. The current explosion of drug abuse and its scientific isolation as a mental disease is a twentieth-century phenomenon and directly related to the unique modernistic stresses of depersonalization and disconnection. As discussed in the previous chapter, Twelve Step programs are effective because they counter these trends by addressing the cultural roots of addiction.

To minister effectively to the addicted, churches need to do the same. In a sense, countering alienation is simply returning to Christianity's foundation. Addicts and alcoholics require a space to be with others in a personal and direct manner, to share their struggles and failures in an open and honest fashion, to receive unconditional acceptance, as well as to be held accountable by people who know their gifts, flaws, and schemes.

There are different ways to create this type of fellowship. One is by offering groups of dedicated purpose. A Bible study, a discipleship class, or a men's or women's group are all possible venues for the type of care that needs to be done, while also familiar parts of a church's program. Less common, but more explicit for the task, would be a group dealing with chronic illnesses or disabilities. For that matter, the church can also offer a group specifically for individuals with alcohol and drug problems.

The more a group is focused upon a specific issue, and the more uncommon it seems, the more important advertising becomes, because its reach must extend beyond the confines of the congregation. Bible studies and women's groups are plentiful in communities, but fellowship for the chronically ill or addicted is not as readily available. These will be groups that serve a deep need in the community and reach people outside the bounds of the church. We must make sure these groups' purposes and schedules are known.

The intention of these groups, in particular, is not to recapitulate a Twelve Step program or a session of AA; rather, these groups are for people with a defining problem who need to meet openly with God and with one another. In that meeting, as people come to know and care for one another, as they jointly share their flaws and victories, God is experienced, and people are empowered. People are the primary channel for the power of God, and connection is the purpose. But such groups require interactive honesty and openness, which are often not aspects of everyday congregational life.

Care needs to be exercised, especially if an effort is made to incorporate these purposes into a Bible study or more familiar church group, to create a context in which addiction or similar issues can be safely discussed. One of my clients, who mentioned her drug use and criminal history in a women's study group, felt very out of place once she broached the issues, feeling like a freak surrounded by straight, middle-class people who could not begin to fathom the life she described. In fact, her admission was probably out of place in a group designed for other purposes. But that also makes the point that the church needs a place, time, and context in which such sharing has a home. Gathering people who have the same or similar difficulties makes the fellowship more likely to respond in a sympathetic and empathic manner. Addicts are very aware of the stigma society attaches to their disorder, and if the church can provide a gathering where that stigma is removed, a very meaningful ministry will be set in motion.

Such a group does not need a highly structured agenda. A prayer, a Bible reading that touches upon a relevant theme, an invitation for people to share their current concerns, and possibly a topic for discussion is all that's needed. The interaction and sharing is more important than the subject matter itself. We can close with the Serenity Prayer[3] and trust that God will be at work.

In my own experience, services devoted to spiritual healing also fit well with the needs of the addicted, while appealing to a broad spectrum of people and incorporating the singular aims of a Christian community. The goal of these gatherings is, again, to bring together an honest encounter with God and between people. Healing occurs in that linkage.

Some basic rules are helpful when starting such a ministry. Keep it simple. Stay away from "mumbo-jumbo." Do not worry about numbers. One week attendance will be large, and the next week, there will be fewer, often because those who are curious come all at once and those who are really interested return. We never make promises for God. We cannot know the mind of God. Rather, we have open-ended faith in God's love and willingness to heal. We keep the focus upon revealing ourselves to God and to one another. It is always an experiment, and what happens is God's work.[4]

We begin with a welcome and an introduction to the group's purposes, followed by a scripture passage, normally dealing with God's power or healings, and a prayer. A short message may be given. We then have time for people to share how God is working in their lives—what goal they achieved this week, the things for which they are grateful—followed by a time for people to share their needs and concerns. Is there a problem they would like to discuss with the group? Encourage interaction, and do not be afraid to ask questions. At the end, we have a time for prayer and a time for silence, giving space for God to act. For those so inclined, we pray while laying hands upon them.

There are many ways to conduct these groups, and people may have ideas of their own. We must simply keep in mind the goal—an experience of unconditional love, honesty, and trust in an environment that brings together people and God. There are no stigmas, only appreciation for the courage that leads someone to share of himself or herself. There is no guilt, only a positive challenge to grow and seek healing. There are no promises, only faith that God will act.

I also strongly recommend conducting occasional groups for drug education. They will help other members learn about drug use and be more comfortable with those who are addicted. A recovering addict within the congregation would be an excellent resource, and books, such as this one, can easily be used. The topic is too important in our current culture to be neglected by the church.

WORSHIP

As the communal gathering for the entire church body, worship carries a symbolic and experiential importance for everyone. Not to feel included is to feel excluded. Unfortunately, the challenges, struggles, experiences, and hopes of the addicted are typically not mentioned during a worship service. Addicts notice such an exclusion, and it becomes part of the reason they feel alienated from the church.

The good news is that this omission can easily be rectified. For example, in prayers, simply including concerns that specifically touch their lives will mean a great deal. Praying for people who have addictions, who are in prison, who are working the streets, who abuse themselves and their bodies, who suffer from domestic violence, who are trying to hold their families together or keep their children away from drugs, are subjects that affect more people than we probably know, yet are often not mentioned. Community prayers, more likely, will touch on these issues in a way that does not speak specifically to the hearts of those who suffer from them.

Sermons are another means of speaking to the addicted. Occasionally we may use themes that come from the Twelve Steps or from the basic keys to recovery. We will find they are topics that preach, have a foundation in the Bible, and speak to everyone. Humility, making amends, taking our own inventory, admitting those things over which we are powerless, or admitting our need for a power based outside ourselves—these are issues that concern or benefit not only addicts, but also many other parishioners. Similarly, when using illustrations or exploring applications of a theme, we can include matters that affect substance abusers. What does the message have to say to people who cannot control themselves or have broken the law or have experienced substantial loss? These are people hungry for a good word but have frequently felt exiled from the community of faith.

However, there is also a significant need for a coherent Christian message that addresses the larger issues of pleasure, the body, the law, and sin. For too long, the church has handed over these extremely important matters to society and to science, allowing opinions that do not consider the will of God to determine the opinions of those who claim to know God's will. As will be discussed in more detail in the next chapter, the morality of drug use involves questions of profound spiritual importance. Yet, by and large, the Christian community has little useful to say, parroting the dominant cultural message, even though much of that message is misleading and institutionally self-serving. Understanding and articulating the Christian perspective of God's will for the twenty-first century, with its increasingly sophisticated interplay of drugs, pleasure, behavioral control, and the manipulation of brain processes, is a requirement if churches desire to remain relevant institutions.

One final thought about worship relates to Communion and the use of wine or juice. I remember very clearly the account of an alcoholic who had attended a Roman Catholic church. After the Eucharist had been served, and the priest drank the remaining wine in the cup, the man found himself struggling with a very strong urge to drink. He saw a priest chugging wine and had a craving to do the same. Church, for him, at that moment, had become unsafe.

An argument can be made that making church unsafe for anyone is unacceptable. If such is the case, using juice, instead of wine, in deference to the alcoholics and drug abusers in a congregation, is an appropriate choice. For those whose theology or tradition mandate wine, offering an option of juice is also suitable. In fact, alcoholics should not drink alcohol of any kind at any time, even during an act of worship. Having a chalice of nonalcoholic juice available is another way that the church can express its recognition and love for those who are recovering from addiction.

---

1. For urine-testing purposes: Marijuana stays in the body for up to thirty days, cocaine and heroin for about three days. Alcohol, being metabolized in a matter of hours, must be tested for soon after being ingested.

2. Jessie Taft, *Otto Rank* (New York: Julian Press, 1958), 139, quoted in Ernest Becker, *The Denial of Death* (New York: Free Press, 1973), 270.

3. "God, grant me the serenity to accept the things I cannot change, the courage to change the things I can, and the wisdom to know the difference."

4. My introduction to this work was from Robert Cartwright, a United Methodist pastor, who had the healers Ambrose and Olga Worrall in his church. His advice and methods are reflected in my own.

4

Morality and Drugs

George was a fifty-three-year-old man who had run his own landscaping business his entire adult life. He was never going to become a millionaire, but he was comfortable and had done well, considering he quit school in the tenth grade. He much preferred working to sitting in a classroom and had been caring for lawns ever since. A gruff but sociable man, George fit the typical image of a hardworking, blue-collar American, except for the fact that he liked to smoke marijuana. Instead of drinking a beer when done for the day, he would light up a joint. He grew marijuana plants for his own use, occasionally giving away the excess he produced to friends who also smoked. He had been doing this for over thirty years.

One day, while taking a pound of pot to a buddy, he was pulled over by the police, who discovered the drugs in his car. Although he had never been in trouble with the law, the amount of marijuana in his possession put him over the limit for pleading to a misdemeanor; instead, he was convicted of a felony and served two years in state prison. Upon release, he was sent to see me because his stipulations stated that he could not use any illegal drugs.

George was a cooperative client who did not return to smoking marijuana because he did not want to break the terms of his parole. But he had difficulty understanding why his life had been interrupted in this drastic fashion. Prison was tough for a first-time offender in his fifties. Apart from his like of marijuana, he had always been a law-abiding citizen. Nor could he understand why marijuana was illegal in the first place. Smoking marijuana was how he relaxed. He equated it with drinking beer and found the whole situation very unfair.

My job in that circumstance was to help him live within the law, whether or not the law made sense. It was simply in his best interests to keep his activities legal. Laws do not have to seem reasonable in order to be enforced, and nobody was asking for his opinion.

At the beginning of the twentieth century, George would not have had this problem. Cannabis, along with every other drug, was legal. In fact, cocaine was the ingredient from which Coca-Cola took its name. Opiates were available in nostrums and elixirs and could be purchased over the counter in drug stores.

A vast change took place in American society, however, with the passage of the Harrison Narcotics Act in 1914, which outlawed both opiates and cocaine. This was followed by the Eighteenth Amendment in 1919, which outlawed the manufacturing or selling of alcoholic beverages, and by the Marijuana Tax Act of 1937, which did the same for marijuana. Even with the repeal of prohibition in 1933, the issue of drug use in the United States had been entirely transformed into one of restriction, illegality, and penal enforcement.

The reasons for this makeover are extremely complex. They involved racism, as particular drugs to be outlawed were identified with feared ethnic groups.[1] They involved the trepidation caused by a quickly growing urban population. They involved dislike of behaviors that ran counter to the values of productivity, moderation, discipline, and predictability.[2] They involved an increasing interest in social reforms and a belief that laws could solve such problems.[3] As political and cultural institutions became involved in the efforts to prohibit drug use, these social anxieties and beliefs were used to pursue institutional agendas, resulting in the bureaucratic, legal, and clinical apparatuses of today's drug enforcement. But, at base, the regulation of drugs and alcohol has been rooted in moral concerns.

The start of a new century is the time to reassess the morality of these issues that, on the local level, result in the incarceration of people like George and decree that he can drink beer but not smoke pot. Rather than stand on the sidelines as scientific, medical, legal, and business interests shape the debate to further their own aims, we need to evaluate drug use from a biblical and Christian perspective and place that perspective into the contemporary discourse.

In this closing chapter, I will frame the discussion of these ideas in a manner that aspires toward a Christian understanding of drug use, intoxication, addiction, and the larger social context of the American drug culture, which includes people like George. Obviously, the discussion will not be exhaustive, but will hopefully provide points of departure for further thought. The drug users within our communities deserve a revised moral compass with which to situate themselves and understand an environment that both judges and encourages drug use.

THE SOCIAL CONTEXT

In approaching this subject, it is important to realize that the concerns run far deeper than whether it is OK to get intoxicated; although, it is a legitimate question that calls for a response. The broader issues, in which the question of intoxication is embedded, go to the heart of power and how power operates in modern society. *For we do not live in a culture that is opposed to the use of drugs.* It is probably safe to say that Americans legally ingest more drugs today than ever before in history. Nor are the drugs prescribed merely antibiotics, although the overuse of antibiotics has been documented. Rather, drugs are increasingly used to change mentality, to control behaviors, to arrange emotions, and to increase productivity. Drugs are used to enhance the adjustment of people otherwise regarded as normal; they are used to help people deal with life challenges otherwise regarded as commonplace.

Examples of such use are all around us: the debates about prescribing Ritalin to schoolchildren; the television ads for psychoactive medications that treat "social anxiety disorder" and simply feeling down; the wide variety of pills to assist with weight loss; the ubiquitous use of the amphetamine caffeine. (Caffeine is what replaced the cocaine in Coca-Cola.) Former senator Bob Dole hawks the same drug that Hugh Hefner credits with allowing him to sexually service several girlfriends while in his seventies.

The point is not that any of these uses are necessarily bad. Rather, I would say we lack a coherent moral standard to judge such uses. The prevailing mores are not intended to provide a consistent standard because, significantly, those mores are not truly about the evils of drug use. If we think that is the case, then we have missed the deeper purposes within the cultural prohibitions.

Those purposes become clearer when we consider how drugs are used as a means to deal with drug abuse. Substituting a synthetic opiate, methadone, for the natural opiate heroin, has taken place in the United States since the 1950s. Methadone, however, is still physically addictive, and withdrawal from methadone is more difficult than withdrawal from heroin. Other drugs are under development for alcohol and cocaine addictions, as well, to chemically block the effects of these substances. In other words, we use drugs to treat drug use.

When the overall picture is surveyed, the primary rationale underlying America's drug policies is not to prevent chemical use or abuse; we legally use and abuse chemicals all the time. Rather, the driving concern is to manage a population. As discussed earlier, the burgeoning capitalist revolution required an increasingly healthy and reliable labor force. That necessity created interest in a hygienics of the social "body," as the populace was viewed, and formulated politico-medical prescriptions that related not only to disease, but also to lifestyle and behavior. The administration of social hygienics has since sought to supervise most aspects of a person's life: food, sexuality, clothing, living space, education, and, fairly recently, drug use.[4]

Managing a population by managing its drug usage begins by attempting to restrict, not drug use, but the portals through which drugs can be accessed. For example, in the nineteenth century, the populace commonly consulted pharmacists about what drugs to use, and pharmacists were able to dispense whatever they thought was appropriate. In fact, they were more commonly known as druggists. In 1906, however, Congress made a physician's written order a requirement for narcotics to be dispensed. Today, opiates (usually in the form of various pain pills) can be obtained for personal use, but a doctor must approve the purchase. Since some doctors dispense these drugs in ample quantities, can be fooled with fake ailments, or do not care, heroin addicts are frequently able to maintain their habits with legitimate drugs. As long as these legitimate drugs are prescribed by doctors, their use is legal as well. Methadone, on the other hand, cannot be dispensed by physicians, but by approved methadone clinics. America's drug policy is not principally about prohibition, but about approved gateways. And gateways are positions of power. The power of the medical profession is derived not primarily from its therapeutic abilities, but from its function as a social hygienist, which gives it sole discretion over many treatments and activities.[5]

The second way that the population is managed in its chemical use is by the invention and prescribing of drugs that affect human conduct with increasing effectiveness and with increasingly predictable results. Once access to drugs has been controlled, at least in theory, the dispensing of drugs to assist in governance can be done with greater efficacy. Behavior modifiers and mood changers can be utilized, but with a form of administrative control that targets specific goals. From this perspective, the problem with street drugs is not that they affect behavior or twist reality, but that they are relatively crude and used outside of approved channels.

For example, the number of people treated for mental or emotional disorders continues to grow, along with the list of what is considered to be a disorder. For these types of problems, the use of drugs has become the dominant form of treatment. Managed care likes drug treatment's cost-effectiveness, and the medical profession believes it offers better outcomes. As a result, psychiatrists are increasingly medication specialists, with others left to do adjustment-oriented counseling.

Alcoholism is a case in point. Regarded at the beginning of the twentieth century as a moral problem, its identity has evolved by stages over the past one hundred years: a moral problem, a psychological problem, a disease, a mental health disorder. Remnants of all these phases echo through the culture and through treatment methods. But the most accepted cutting-edge views are that addiction is a form of mental illness with an organic base or a chronic brain disease, which is the same thing. Treating addicts with drug therapy is then the logical choice, offering the best prognosis, until the day comes when genetic engineering may offer a true cure.

From the perspective of its methods and aims, America's drug program is about governance of a large and unruly population, in both a restrictive and proactive manner. It is not just about the drugs that are proscribed, but also about the ones that are prescribed. Understanding this fact is important before attempting to establish a coherent morality, especially for people who have accepted the drug regulations as the equivalent of a moral system. The inconsistencies within the regulations belie that common assumption. George could legally get drunk seven days a week, for example, but not smoke pot. The rules are capricious as a form of moral order because their underlying logic is not based on an overall or controlling belief—for example, that drug use is offensive.

People often assume the regulatory program represents a supervening moral perspective, since the original impetus for regulation came from moralistic concerns. However, the rules are the product of institutional interests; they are management vehicles.

Understanding these aims is important because it makes clear that a coherent moral standard for drug consumption must address drugs' legal uses, and not just restrictions. Not to understand them would be a serious mistake, considering the ever enlarging pharmacopoeia used upon an ever growing segment of the population for an ever increasing profit. Any useful morality must include the acceptable-drug-using culture, rather than merely moralize about those who get intoxicated or use illegal substances. Why does the term "druggie" seem applicable only to illegal drug users? In fact, the legal uses of drugs can be more profoundly troubling than the trafficking and use of illegal chemicals. To ignore that morally, as Jesus said, is like straining out the gnat while swallowing the camel.

THE MATERIALIST PROGRAM

Questions about the accepted uses for psychoactive substances concern more than these substances' ability to alter or manipulate processes in the brain. It can be argued that there are people for whom these manipulations offer a measure of relief. The trouble goes deeper, to science and the positivist drug culture's assumed view of the person. It is a view that reduces human experience to a materialist basis, representing the human body as a machine and human behaviors as mechanical activities operated by an electrochemical system. The nonmaterial aspects of human consciousness are discounted as secondary qualities; quantifiable intelligence is touted, instead, as the measure of a human. The brain is approached as an organic form of computer, and the day is foreseen when inorganic computers will simulate and surpass human intelligence.[6] At that point, the difference between humans and machines may be blurred, if not irrelevant.

If we pay attention, we see that cultural images of humans as machines fill the media and inform us in a variety of ways. It may be as blatant as implanting an artificial heart, or as subtle as using human embryos for the production of stem cells. But, as images, they are not value-free.

This biotechnological model of a person leads to a behaviorist perception of human actions. For example, any particular behavior is thought to be determined by external stimuli and conditioned response, learned and repeated firing patterns within the brain's neuronic circuits. This, in turn, sets up a functional relationship between the brain and the mind,[7] in which the human mind is known solely by behaviors or dispositions to behavior. In essence, the mind does not exist except as observed or measured activities.

In this way, human consciousness is dismissed as nothing more than the sum of its behaviors. There are no value-added ingredients. That which has made consciousness appear sacred is rejected. What is experienced as a unique self that witnesses and knows the surrounding world is the product of coordinated brain circuitry, operating on a subpersonal level to construct an orderly flow of thought: "What is illusory or mistaken is only the view that I am some distinct substantial self who produces these connections in virtue of a totally non-behavioral form of understanding."[8]

From this perspective, maladaptive patterns of behavior or repeated emotional maladjustments are produced by abnormalities within the brain's circuitry, or the learned programs. There is nothing else to blame beyond the wires and the way they are hooked up; any other form of influence or power is denied. Since the wiring is an electrochemical operation, chemicals are the most appropriate manner to redress the malfunctions or intervene in the dysfunctional programs. Because there is no self apart from the action of these circuits, no self that surpasses the chemical processes or exists on a different level of being, there are no quandaries about chemically manipulating the self or producing artificial experiences or inhibiting real ones. In a sense, all experience is artificial. Reality is chemically produced.

This biotechnological model of the human person is what underlies the modern positivist practice of drug therapeutics and allows the scientific and medical communities to believe they can successfully redirect brain activities. But it is also the dark heart of the modern drug culture. The cynicism of its worldview leaves no standards by which to judge human functioning, apart from the prevailing social norms. As such, it is technology perfectly suited for the management of a population. But a sense of the sacred is removed. There is no spiritual transcendence. And reality can be changed with a pill.

This means it is also a worldview perfectly suited to encourage drug use, and modern America reflects that fact. Substance abusers live in a culture that promotes the use of chemicals and provides ready-made rationales for using drugs. Unfortunately for the aims of management, that encouragement does not simply lead to using legal drugs and prescribed medications.

A television ad for an antidepressant shows a woman staring out a window at an Edenic summer day. The implication of the image is that use of this medication will change the world; it's a visual reminder of the message that chemicals can produce reality. The stated intention of the medication is to help someone cope; the presentation is of a miraculous transformation. Beer commercials will often push the same idea: "You, too, can live in a world of beautiful people, nice cars, and intense fun." A cigarette ad shows a group of twenty-somethings, with white teeth and beaming smiles, beside the caption "Alive with Pleasure."

Chemicals, of course, do not bring about this transformation. The experiential source of depression will remain, assuming that life experiences can be traumatic and cause depression, until the difficult emotional issues have been resolved. But a pill offers otherwise. Transcendence, in our culture, is increasingly becoming a chemical one. Rather than change the world or rise above it, we can manipulate our brains to change our experience of the world.

This is also a frequent refrain among the substance abusers and addicts in treatment. They want that summer day and choose among a wide variety of chemicals obtained by prescription or off the street, often acting as amateur chemists, hoping to alter the world in which they find themselves. It is a strategy that has been taught to them and that they view as a legitimate endeavor. It is not surprising that those who lack enough money to find a doctor willing to provide what they wish resort to other means. It is also not surprising that they are often attracted to drugs with some intoxicating properties, most of which are controlled or illegal.

When the drugs fail, people are left without resources. They will most often use more drugs or different drugs, hoping that something will be different this time. But where there is no hope of surpassing the materiality of their lives, ultimately nothing matters, which is what drug users believe in the end. Life is mechanics, not connections. Nothing is sacred. Get what you can. Try to relieve the boredom or despair with chemicals again. That is the cyclical nature of the drug culture and is reflected in much of modern American society.

BIBLICAL PERSPECTIVES

Alcohol and drugs were known and used in the ancient world. The Egyptians and Assyrians drank beer. The Greeks and Romans drank wine, which is also the alcoholic drink mentioned in the Bible.[9] The Hebrews commonly used fermented grape juice, although wine produced from dates and pomegranates was common in other cultures, and there's little question that it was intoxicating. Numerous scripture passages warn against drunkenness, but there are passages that also extol moderate use: "Wine can put new life into you if you drink it in moderation. What would life be like without it? Wine was created to make us happy. If you drink it in moderation and at the right time, it can lift your spirits and make you cheerful" (Sirach 31:27-28 TEV).

In the New Testament, Jesus turned water into some very fine wine, which implies he knew what fine wine was like. Later, when he is accused of being a glutton and a drunkard, he does not rebut the indictment. That does not mean he was an alcoholic; he most likely did not find the charge important enough to merit a response. Instead, Jesus counsels against eating, drinking, or worrying too much, as examples of how our attention can be distracted from seeking the Kingdom (Luke 21:34).

Opiates were also well known in biblical times, first being referred to in Homer's *Odyssey* as a drug that "quiets all pains and quarrels." The *Materia Medica* of Discorides (c. A.D. 70) summarizes the many therapeutic uses of opium. Marcus Aurelius consumed opium daily, adjusting the dose according to whether he wanted to sleep or feel good.[10] Considering the length of time that Greek and Roman culture occupied Palestine, and the effectiveness of opium for relieving pain, it is hard to believe that opiate use was not imported into Hebrew practices, even though the Bible never mentions it.

When the Bible is surveyed, what becomes evident is that the perils of substance abuse do not merit a lot of direct consideration. There are warnings about excess use. Noah is used as a cautionary example of drunkenness (Gen. 9:20-27), but there is no such person as an alcoholic or an addict. They are not even a category of sinner; they are not included with tax collectors and prostitutes. Drunks are regarded as foolish or irresponsible, not deviates or criminals. If we are looking to find a scriptural basis for the current drug regulations and program, it is not there.

However, looking to the Bible to support the current restrictions would be a superficial approach to the Bible, as well as to drug users and the American drug culture. As already discussed, drug use does not take place in isolation, and abusers cannot properly be situated apart from their cultural context. Neither can they be situated apart from the context of their other patterns of behavior. Formulating a new morality for the issue of drug use in contemporary society requires leaving people in context, in their relations and connections, and it is here that the Bible begins to speak.

One of the reasons that the modern concept of an addict as diseased or having a mental disorder does not appear in the Bible is that the modern view of a human is often incompatible with a biblical one. The materialist program analyzes a person as a system of interactive components, locating the source of a dysfunction as self-contained within that system. When we are sick, we are sick alone, in the sense that the illness is segregated within. A good analogy would be of a cancer, in which the disease is an isolated, autonomous growth within the larger body. Humans with disease or mental illness are treated as tumors, where the disorder is discrete and isolated from any larger context, be it cultural or cosmic. Say what we like about societal causes for various kinds of deviance or disease, that's not the way they are treated. Disorder is quarantined metaphorically and physically.

Illness, in this sense, is unknown in the Bible. Disorders were understood within a hierarchical network of relationships. What we casually assume was a superstitious and naïve belief in possession and spiritual forces was, more profoundly, a view that disorder arises within disruptions, imbalances, and trespasses in fields of reciprocal relations. Illness extends outward from the person, eventually reaching connections with incomprehensible powers, just as illness is also a marker for how those relationships return, so that no one is ill alone or in isolation. The human stands at the center of a universe of attention, and dysfunction occurs within the whole. Even lepers, while feared and shunned, were not believed to be the detached and solitary site of their own disease. Rather, they were considered unclean, which connected their affliction to boundaries and powers that ran through the entire cosmos. Remission was a sign of having been rendered clean by God.

Echoes of this ancient form of thinking can be found in the manner that people often search for explanations concerning illness or death. They ask, What did I do to deserve this? and Why do bad things happen to good people? These thoughts reveal a belief that people and their disorders are linked to larger issues, to relationships, boundaries, and a universe of forces, in which the body and self are immersed.

Unfortunately, these questions often result in guilt because they lack the ancient framework of thought that makes them intelligible. Most notable is the biblical idea that the universe is a living creation, imbued with awareness, more akin to an organism than a machine. This principle underlays all the miracle stories and the numerous times the world is shown as responding to human activity. It is the conception that makes intercessory prayer comprehensible and more than wishful thinking. It is why Paul sees all of creation, not just humanity, as subjected to futility, longing for deliverance, and groaning with the pains of childbirth (Rom. 8:19-22). There is unity in the cosmos that is a reflection of God's nature and results in a living, knowing, and loving universe.[11] Nothing more deeply underscores the vast difference between biblical thinking and much of modern thought.

The biotechnological model holds consciousness to be a production of neural networks that developed because it provided an evolutionary advantage. Humans are mechanisms at the service of genes and their evolutionary needs; there is no higher purpose than the unfolding of genetic code. In the biblical model, all of creation, and human life in particular, is an expression of God, who seeks to bring that expression into a fuller awareness and reflection of its source. We live because we are in relationship with God, with the cosmos, and with each other. The development of those relationships, along with the awareness and love they require, is the highest purpose.

Attempts to understand, from a biblical perspective, human health and disorder begin with the place of the human in a web of relationships that is both local and cosmic. They do not begin by attempting to diagnose the mechanical problem. Treating people as if fixing a car may mend certain problems, but it perpetuates deeper ones. One of the gifts of the Twelve Step program, and a sign of its biblical base, is the way it demonstrates the importance of relationship and connection and the disease of alienation. Most deeply, health and disorder are a matter of mind and heart, of awareness and love, and of the relationships of which these consist.

Asking the question, "What did I do to deserve this?" is not silly or simple-minded. It is a search for relationships in a modern world that lacks them. What is missing is a sense of order in the cosmos and a person's place, both large and small; there is little understanding of a person's connection to what lies beyond and the roots of his or her life. Developing those connections and roots, in the biblical sense, is the purpose of a morality or moral order. When we seek a revised moral compass for the use of drugs in modern society, the goal is to place drug use within that context and within life's relationships.

MORAL DIRECTIONS

This discussion about the purposes of the positivist drug culture, its inherent perspective about the nature of a human being, and its profound differences with a biblical view, suggest several areas where a revised morality can begin. Perhaps, with thought, the Christian community will be able to offer a new framework in which drug users can understand themselves and their society and find support for a life without drug abuse.

1. *Morality is about vision.* "Where there is no vision the people get out of hand; happy are they who keep the law" (Prov. 29:18 NJB).

This piece of wisdom literature indicates the importance of understanding our place in creation and the relationships that sustain us. The conduct of people is not effectively determined by rules, but by a revelation from which flows the manner that we live our lives. Those happy in the law are those who know the law as what opens us more deeply to the source of life. That vision is the foundation of morality.

This is very different from the use of morality as a social tool, the purpose of which is to have a disciplinary impact upon its members, to exert a controlling force and authority upon individual minds. In the thought of someone like Emile Durkheim, this disciplinary force was the source of social order, of civilization, and, subsequently, of the human animal.[12] It is not necessary that these moral systems correspond with external reality in any direct fashion. In fact, as has been discussed, it is doubted whether reality is directly apprehended. Rather, "social order exists *only* as a product of human activity," even when humans think it is "something other than a human product."[13]

Constructed in an ongoing manner by the operation of social forces, cultural morality reflects institutional aims, including those of institutionalized religion, as those institutions align themselves. That is what accounts for their ad hoc appearance. George cannot smoke marijuana or use cocaine, but he can smoke cigarettes and get drunk. Illegal drugs are made legal with a properly authorized piece of paper. The money spent on the enforcement of drug laws does little to prevent illegal drug use.

This is not morality of a higher order. The purpose is about management of a population and is why, in modern societies, moral vision is subsumed by regulation. Efficacy lies in the success of imposing orderliness, as determined by institutional goals.

Jesus turns this order around. In a statement very pertinent to modern practices, Jesus says the law is subsumed by love (Matt. 22:37-40). The law, from his perspective, is not about regulation or institutional agendas; it is about fulfilling the purposes for which humans were created. That is the vision. For Christians, the foundation of morality is love, not control and management.

In developing a moral understanding for the use of drugs, love is where one should begin. That may sound trite, but it's amazing how often the Christian community fails to embark from that place. The first stance to take in regard to drug users and abusers is one of love; they have a place among us. They are not moral exiles. Even if they are actively using substances, especially as lost souls, they have a place among the people of God because that community includes everyone.

When talking with clients about how to recognize a higher power that can offer true empowerment, I always emphasize that a higher power accepts unconditionally. A higher power operates through meetings of AA or NA because addicts know they will be received in exactly that manner. No matter what they share, no one will head for the door. If they arrive high or drunk, they will not be turned out; they will be asked to sit quietly. A morality concerning drug abuse begins with love.

Many addicts, and the unchurched in general, often have a different experience in church. They feel out of place, in part because of their own insecurity and guilt. Their life circumstances may have left them unable to dress correctly. They see people surrounded by families, while their own may be dysfunctional or abandoned.

They will never feel at home, and healing cannot begin until they bring their darkest secrets before God and we tell them that they belong. And those secrets may include their continuing drug use or returning to drug use, even after bringing themselves to God. Recovery is a process, and love accepts it as such. All of us, after all, are on that long and winding road.

2. *Morality is about accepting relationships.* "Neither do I condemn you. Go away, and from this moment sin no more" (John 8:11 NJB).

These words of Jesus, to a woman caught in the act of adultery, are remarkably challenging. Like his teaching about loving our enemies, his words can seem to be highly impractical. "Loving our enemies" is likely to get us killed. "Letting sinners or criminals go free" will lead to social anarchy. Before we fall into those traps of thinking, however, let's recognize that Jesus is teaching an orientation toward people. He is demonstrating a manner of relating.

As I have illustrated with the cases of actual people, drug addicts can do some awful things. I have dealt with clients who had sex with their own children, killed people, stole possessions from their grandmothers, committed rape, engaged in straight and gay prostitution, and left behind a string of unwanted kids. But the moral vision being outlined requires a posture of love and acceptance towards these people, based upon the idea that the only difference between us is one of degree. Elsewhere, Jesus reduces the distinction between engaging in adultery and simply thinking about it. All humans live on the same spectrum of behavior; no one is beyond our kin.

This does not mean we should ignore someone's behaviors or pretend there is no such thing as sin. Addicts require honesty in order to see themselves and the consequences of their actions. Jesus acknowledged the woman's sin at the same time that he did not judge her. It is important to speak uncomfortable words. But honesty exists only when it is not accompanied by personal judgment. Otherwise, it becomes manipulation.

When I was in the parish ministry, a very active parishioner confessed to me that he was involved in an extramarital relationship. Despite our talks, his affair continued for months, which made me very uncomfortable. Finally, I said he was not welcome in the church until he stopped. It is a decision I regret, in part because of the attempted manipulation. I was reacting to the fears his actions prompted in me and tried to punish him accordingly. Continued honesty was called for, not condemnation or retribution.

An important reason to address this issue, in a revised moral understanding, is that our culture's primary response to illegal addiction is punitive. For institutional reasons, that have little to do with effectively handling the use of illegal drugs, incarceration and enforcement remain the dominant form of treatment. Prisons are full of addicts and street-corner dealers, who often sell to maintain their own habits. Drug use continues unabated; unfortunately, when one dealer is removed, another immediately takes his or her place.

Without question, many people feel satisfied when users and dealers are placed in prison. But that satisfaction is the attitude that a revised morality about drug abuse needs to replace. It is a stance that has nothing to do with effecting change and everything to do with personal fears. Guilt, banishment, pain, and shame are not experiences that prevent someone from using drugs; rather, they encourage it. Bringing people together and giving addicts a face, in the moral environment a church can offer, is the most likely way that this desire to punish can be exchanged for a posture of love. In the end, everyone moves closer to the Kingdom.

Reducing the desire to punish also speaks a moral word to our dominant cultural practices. The enforcement measures that affect our communities have much more to do with the distribution of money, the preservation of positions, and the administration of certain groups of people, than with the actual care of people. From a biblical perspective, those measures and their motivations are examples of immorality. Immorality, most deeply, is not about breaking rules; it's about failing to love. It is about elevating money and power and fear over the human. Immorality punishes, rather than helps others see themselves and change.

3. Morality deals with the whole. "Human beings live not on bread alone but on every word that comes from the mouth of God" (Matt. 4:4 NJB).

In this statement, Jesus was not devaluing the importance of food. He was insisting on not being sidetracked by singular issues, or being misled by a concern for the particular, when the need is for an embracing vision. The particular and singular can be situated only within the whole.

This aspect of a moral vision presents a challenge to the materialist program within our culture. The strategy of materialism is to break things down into increasingly small and discrete parts that are more amenable to being handled and controlled. From the parts, categorizations are made, taxonomies constructed, and processes defined. As I have discussed, the brain is deconstructed into circuits, the circuits into neurons, the neurons into cells, the cells into chemical operations, and the chemicals into formulaic reactions. It is from this minute perspective that science makes claims about understanding the brain and attempts to meddle in its operations.

From the standpoint of the statement of Jesus, those are foolhardy claims. It is not so much failing to see the forest for the trees, but failing to see the trees because of their molecular activity, let alone see the forest. It is like an astronomer who thinks the universe is understood because the stars have been counted or the total amount of energy quantified, without asking why it exists in the first place.

Some of the roots of this approach to the world can be traced back to the sixteenth-century philosopher Rene Descartes and his desire for certainty. Beginning with himself—"I think, therefore I am"—Descartes proceeded to build a new view of the world that equated certitude with truth. As summarized by Karl Mannheim, "Only that has validity which I can control in my own perception, which is corroborated in my own experimental activity, or which I myself can produce or at least conceptually construct as producible."[14]

One of the results of such assumptions, however, is that mystery is avoided, not because mystery has nothing to teach, but because it escapes the need for certainty and control. Dealing with the body as a collection of organs and mechanical processes delivers benefits within the limits of its purview. Some diseases are eliminated; others no longer prove fatal. Life expectancy lengthens. Infant mortality rates decline. But people still become sick, and new diseases arise. Tragedy continues to occur, and evil persists, as revealed most bluntly by the World Trade Center and Pentagon devastation. The obsession with control evades the inscrutability presented by the body and by life, and by the revelation that certainty of the materialist kind is impossible.

Nevertheless, the endeavor does have an impact upon perceptions of the world and people. A materialist form of economics, for example, sees people as units or as production capacity. A materialist science sees the world as a machine and the brain as a computer. A materialist form of medicine sees life as the state of a body that is not dead, and disease as a constellation of measurable symptoms.

This approach to the human is what pulls people who abuse substances out of their living context and analyzes them according to specific signs of maladjustment. However, there is a sense in which individuals who are clinically or psychiatrically evaluated feel alienated from the process and themselves. They are placed within a mental health taxonomy, which isolates particular behaviors and, by so doing, believes some form of certainty and control has been gained.

What is lost is viewing that same conduct within a fuller picture of the person and of general human action. For example, all human activity belongs to various patterns of behaviors. Everything we do falls into some form of repetitious conduct, whether that conduct is subtle or dominant and ruling. In other words, all of us manifest habitual behaviors in a wide variety of ways. But, our dominant patterns will not be harmful ones. However, if they are, we will have trouble breaking free. The behavior of an abused spouse who habitually returns to live with her abuser can be just as heartbreaking, and difficult to change, as the behavior of one who habitually injects heroin. From this perspective, addiction is a damaging and dominating version of the more mundane habits found among everyone. Addicts are not different in kind.

That manner of perceiving the drug addicts within our midst, viewing them as a whole and within the whole of the human family, reflects Christian morality. They are not specimens; they are people with proclivities like us all. They are not abnormal but clearly part of the whole of humanity, reflecting the singular manner in which humans behave, even if tragically.

This encompassing perception, and its essential role within morality, is also a challenge to the substance abusers themselves. The most compelling and personal reason to stop using a drug is if it presents a pattern of interference. That pattern of interference can be fully recognized only with a comprehensive examination of a person's life. But addicted persons often try to avoid that kind of total examination by their own focus upon the particulars. It is a common strategy for fleeing reality.

Substance users, as well, need to be held to this moral standard as a means of evaluating themselves, since it reveals the crux of abuse. The questions cannot be limited to whether the drugs were legal or how much was used. Justifications that appeal to excerpted aspects of life cannot be accepted. The framework is the whole, the fullness of the environment in which people live. To help people face that kind of larger look at themselves, to help them deal with the guilt or shame it can engender, may require ministry. But in the end, it is a necessary examination to make.

Does George's regular use of pot truly cause no problems, as he believes, apart from its unreasonable illegality? He asserts that he works every day, but has he been injured by being less aware? His wife does not complain, but does smoking every evening leave him disconnected from his partner? He has a comfortable life, but has he stopped growing emotionally and spiritually because the daily use of pot makes him not care? It helps him relax, but why has he not learned other methods for handling his stress? If he likes his life, as he claims, why does he regularly use a carcinogen?

It is possible to use some drugs in a sociable, healthy, and recreational manner. But the morality of that use requires an encompassing assessment. It is a stringent standard. From this perspective, drug use becomes immoral when it repeatedly damages anything within the entire circumference of our lives. That is when drug use can be called a sin, including the sin of repeatedly failing to examine ourselves seriously.

4. *Morality is concerned with what we know.* "I am the good shepherd; I know my own and my own know me" (John 10:14 NJB).

These words of Jesus succinctly capture the heart of the Christian message. To know, as spoken by Jesus, means far more than a simple cognition of facts. Knowing involves relationship, awareness, and love. Knowing forms the core of the Christian vision concerning God, life, and creation.

Knowing, in this sense, is rooted in Hebrew thought. For the Hebrews, knowledge was not achieved by an objective assessment of external reality. Rather, knowledge was found in the relations and incidents of life. It was revealed by history. It was personal. To know someone, whether as God or as a person, was to be intimately involved.[15]

Since the Hebrews started with the universal, of which the individual person was a manifestation (unlike Platonic thought, which started with the particular and worked outward to the more general and abstract), knowing is an act of reciprocal intimacy. God knows us, which also calls for a knowing response—to be aware, to care, and to live the kind of life that accords with such knowledge. It is through this search to know God and the world around us that people come to know themselves most deeply. To know is also to know we are known, that we belong and have a purpose. We exist in relationship with all of creation. Death is the alienation that results from not knowing or not seeking to know. God calls us to live in community because it is an essential aspect of human life. The church, in particular, is intended to be a community that nurtures a knowing response.

However, this relational and personal knowledge can be developed only by humans in a practical manner, with the tools we have at hand. We have been called into being within a particular domain, and it is here that we work out the meaning of our call. A moral vision provides the guidance for pursuing that purpose within this world, among the other beings created by God. Biblical morality, in this profound sense, concerns what we know, and the issue of drug usage must be addressed from that point of view.

The difference between this biblical perspective and a modernist, technological viewpoint is best revealed by a comparison of "knowing" with the scientific term "consciousness." Consciousness, as I've already discussed, is understood to be the product of advanced processes in the brain that create the illusion of being a distinct entity apart from that neural-chemical circuitry. All knowledge, as well, is produced by these same circuits, so that our personalized experience of the world can be described as a virtual form of reality, internally generated, and not greatly different from the current cutting edge of video games, which present a total sensory immersion.[16] In fact, sophisticated video games are an apt analogy for how this type of science views human experience and for why researchers in artificial intelligence believe that human thought can be duplicated in machines. Accordingly, adjusting brain processes with chemicals is akin to adjusting game processors to achieve better play or to correct malfunctions.

The differing moral implications of these divergent viewpoints is clear. Biblical morality is concerned with our ability to know because that is our deepest human purpose. Not only is there something to know, but also we exist in a living relationship of knowing and being known. Our Creator calls for response. A technological approach sees no higher purpose than making a better adjustment to the surrounding environment, because that is the way of greatest productivity and least stress. People do not belong; they fit in, which also becomes the moral aim.

It is by understanding the biblical perception, and its difference from a technological approach, that we can best address both the proscription and the prescription of drugs. Their legal and illegal uses raise moral concerns, since they involve a faculty that the Bible regards as a salient human trait—the ability to know and respond, to God and others, with our whole being. Anything that enhances or diminishes that ability is a moral issue. With that in mind, chronic intoxication raises obvious problems. It is hard to know anything, especially in any spiritual sense, when frequently drunk or high. But even if drug use is labeled as therapeutic, upon closer analysis, we found a complex mixture of motivations and results that fall under the rubric of governance. Psychiatric drug therapies are designed to help people function within institutional definitions of normalcy. And normalcy is not the same as a knowing response.

For example, one of the problems with the therapeutic use of drugs is the basic definition of an illness that requires such treatment. Although this may seem relatively simple, because we have been indoctrinated with the categories of psychiatric thought, the characterization of mental illness clearly reflects cultural values. Behaviors that in pre-modern societies might have qualified someone as a prophet or a shaman, such as hearing a voice or falling into a trance, could today qualify that person as disordered. Ecstatic behaviors and the reception of divine revelation are common activities in religious history but are regarded with a great deal of suspicion, if not plainly labeled pathological, by the scientific community. Francis of Assisi, Saint Teresa, and Joan of Arc would have been offered medication.

Just as instructive can be the divergent diagnostic conclusions found within contemporary cultures with different ideological foundations. In Communist China, mental illness is claimed not to exist except as an infection of the Western world. Professor Suh Tsung-hwa, a Chinese psychiatrist, has observed that "neuroses and psychoses do not exist here, not even paranoia. At the bottom of these neuroses—a bourgeois sickness—is egoism. In the West, egoism is necessary for survival."[17] While the influence of Chinese ideology upon mental health diagnoses seems clear, the influence of Western ideology upon our own diagnostics also occurs, but in a way to which we often are blind.

Because of these cultural and institutional biases, what is being treated with drugs is not an incapacitating disorder, in many instances, but nonconformity. That is the underlying cultural purpose, as populations are managed, assisted by a technology that lacks guidelines other than those imposed by a culture. However, if nonconformity is associated with people who have special knowledge, or who know in a remarkably direct manner, as is often the case in the Bible, then the morality of using drugs for the purpose of conformity can be questioned. It can be called a form of mind-control that inhibits the freedom granted with awareness.

A similar moral issue is raised by the manner in which awareness can be chemically manipulated. As pointed out earlier, rather than deal with the exigencies of life by developing a more sensitive and refined awareness, by seeking to know God and our place in the world, we can use chemicals to synthetically alter perception. The search to know, the need to be intimately related, may be derailed by a drug-induced perspective that diminishes the felt impact of problems or simply makes people not care. As a result, growth-inducing and even life-changing struggle can be circumvented by the convenience of a drug.

The psychiatrist Alfred Adler believed that mental illness was an existential, not a biological, problem: "Neurosis and psychosis are modes of expression for human beings who have lost courage."[18] From this point of view, mental illness is really a problem caused by the failure to transcend material existence.[19] In that case, if illness is most often a loss of courage and a failure to find a spiritual transcendence, then drug use, whether legal or illegal, can easily become an accomplice in further failure. It is not hard to imagine a "brave new world," in which all forms of existential pain can be chemically muted and all forms of pleasure can be chemically induced. Nor is it hard to imagine the terrible impact that practice would have upon the growth and health of humanity.

On an individual level, this moral question confronts drug users in the deepest possible manner. It is one thing to have drugs available, either by prescription or by illegal channels, but the decision to take them is usually a personal choice. Even when they are recommended by a doctor, most people still can decide whether to comply with the recommendation. The rock musician Scott Weiland, who was diagnosed with bipolar disorder, nevertheless chooses not to take the drugs he was given. He explains:

> Yeah, I've had it my whole life, but it wasn't diagnosed correctly until about three years ago. I finally had a bunch of tests taken—hours and hours of tests. And the medication I was prescribed worked. The thing was, I didn't like the effects of it, so I don't take it. I don't have fear of writing songs without being under the influence of narcotics or alcohol, but I have an incredible fear of writing songs without being able to feel my full range of emotions.[20]

The choice he describes is a moral one, in a biblical sense, since it involves both his ability to know and to express what he knows. When drugs offer to make life easier, however, making the same decision as Weiland can be difficult. Should I take the antidepressant because I function better when I am less burdened by my thoughts and feelings? Should I take the antipsychotic medication because it makes the voices I hear stop talking? Should I smoke marijuana because it helps me relax? Using the biblical importance attached to the act of knowing, a few guidelines can be suggested.

One guideline is that drugs can be positive and useful when a mental dysfunction chronically interrupts a person's ability to know. Such a person often becomes a danger to himself or herself or to others, and medical science can offer some relief. Rolando was a client who suffered from extreme psychosis, which ultimately required hospitalization. He saw monsters and heard voices that continually told him to hurt himself. He saw excrement covering everything. There were days he was unable to make himself sit down, standing upright until his feet were swollen and he was in a great deal of pain. Medication did help control these mental tortures, and he became a cogent, pleasant young man, able to relate and know the world around him. Jesus performed a similar action, without drugs, with the Gerasene demoniac (Mark 5:1-15). Fortunately, such severe cases are rare. But, in these uncommon situations drugs can restore a knowing faculty and may be life-saving medication, like insulin for a diabetic, that is required for the rest of a person's life.

A second guideline might suggest that drugs can offer positive benefits when used on a short-term or occasional basis. When an emotional crisis or a disruptive behavior pattern interferes with our ability to relate to others, and so also interferes with moving ahead in our lives, medication may provide temporary aid. Drugs can help a person get out of bed in the morning or help stabilize mood swings between depression and mania or help relieve physical pain. But the goal must be to address our problems in a more direct and personal manner: to know ourselves, to know our patterns, to know our bodies, to know our depression, to know our fears, to know our pain, to know our relationships with the world around us, to know God. It is in that way that we are able eventually to transcend the very real tribulations that threaten to disable us.

The danger is that drugs can prevent that difficult work from occurring. It is not unusual, and may be the norm, for people who take medication in this manner to remain on them for a very long time. Doctors often prescribe them without any thought for encouraging their clients, or encouraging our society, to deal with the underlying issues. It is easier, for example, to take Prozac than it is to delve into the swamp of emotions that may lurk in the back of our minds. It is easier to hand out opiates for chronic pain, and frequently create addicts, than it is to help people learn non-drug methods for pain management. It is far easier to hand out Ritalin than it is to confront the fact that American classrooms are primarily designed to teach only a certain kind of student. This is how America's drug culture works itself out on a local and personal level, even as we stigmatize people whose drug of choice is illegal.

Unfortunately, for people whose awareness falls outside the norms of culture, there are few alternatives to drugs for handling the problems they face, especially for people who lack money. Presumably the rock musician Scott Weiland has adequate funds to care for himself and is in an industry that allows for nonconformity. But as managed care reduces funds for all kinds of psychotherapy and finds drug therapy cost-effective, people on private insurance and Medicaid will have increasingly little choice. They can deal with ostracism, incapacity, and even forced hospitalization, or enter psychiatric treatment. That, in itself, is a moral issue for the Christian community to consider in our drug-using culture.

It is within this context that we can best address the experience of intoxication, the issue where moralizing about drug use began. We have already noted Bible passages that commend the use of wine, when used moderately and at appropriate times, for its ability to make people cheerful. Even the Puritans, on whom we place blame for excessive moralizing, did not outlaw intoxicants. According to the *Mayflower*'s log, the ship landed at Plymouth because food had run short, "especially our bere."[21] The Pilgrims consumed, and presumably felt the effects of, alcohol from time to time.

As the Bible and much of Christian tradition would indicate, the morality or immorality of intoxication is not primarily a matter of how a particular drug makes us feel. The feeling of intoxication is itself a fluid affair. Does intoxication refer to feeling "buzzed," or does it mean falling down drunk? Is the chronic alcoholic who does not feel drunk after drinking a twelve-pack less intoxicated than the neophyte who feels "loopy" after two cans? When Paul recommended wine to Timothy, did he mean that wine was acceptable as long as Timothy did not feel anything (1 Tim. 5:23)?

It is much more fruitful to analyze this issue with the same guidelines applied to prescribed medication. The concern is that our faculty to know and intimately relate not be diminished or compromised. Short-term or occasional use, which could include the moderate use of intoxicants (alcohol, amphetamines, cannabis, cocaine, opiates), does not significantly impair our abilities and can even "gladden the heart" now and then. The problem is when usage becomes chronic and immoderate. Even more, because of their nature, intoxicants make these problems much worse.

As noted earlier, the body develops tolerance to the effects of intoxicants, so that people end up chasing a euphoria that requires greater amounts used more often. But the greater amounts consumed end up being necessary simply to feel normal, as the body and mind adapt to the regular use of a drug. At this point, as people fall into the throes of drug abuse, they become largely unconscious creatures. They are aware of little beyond the chemical manipulations they chase and, as a result, cause an enormous amount of damage to everyone around them.

Some drugs are more likely than others to lead to this destructive whirlpool. Alcohol and marijuana, for example, despite the ways they can interfere with a life, are relatively mild intoxicants that generally require a fair amount of time to become problematic. Crack, by way of contrast, is an intense intoxicant whose effect is to make a person feel like a god for fifteen seconds. Heroin leaves a person feeling profoundly sheltered, as if wrapped in a cocoon or a womb. Speed can leave people feeling incredibly alive, euphoric, and energetic for up to six hours at a time. They all are difficult drugs to take moderately or to experience mildly. Their intense intoxication ultimately skews a person's awareness, so that awareness accompanying daily reality appears boring and very unappealing. A common result, in that case, is chronic intoxication. A person desires to be high throughout the day; normal activities seem more interesting or more bearable while one is intoxicated. Addiction is born.

When that occurs—and it can occur with any drug—drug use has again ceased to be moral. But since particular drugs make that result almost inevitable, because of their intensity, there is good reason to view their recreational use as always morally suspect. We can decide, of course, that any use of intoxicants is morally wrong simply because of the millions of people who are harmed by them. Paul suggests that as an ethical choice (Rom. 14:21). In choosing that approach, however, we need to remember that the issue is far more than merely the immorality of illegal substances. The use of drugs in Paul's time was nothing like our own.

In the end, we need to keep in mind that this is an issue upon which people—including Christians—can legitimately disagree and that community remains more important than being right. During seminary I worked as a pastoral intern at an Episcopal church. Raised as a United Methodist, I was surprised when I showed up for my first church supper and discovered that Episcopalians could bring wine and beer to the meal. But nobody got drunk, God did not seem scandalized, and it did not diminish the warm fellowship they had with one another. The issues are serious and the damages very real, but love is the essence of our identity.

---

1. Cocaine was believed to make the African American population more dangerous, for example, and opium was linked to Asians as a culturally subversive group.

2. H. Wayne Morgan, *Drugs in America: A Social History, 1800–1980* (Syracuse, N.Y.: Syracuse University Press, 1981), 62.

3. Jean Kinney and Gwen Leaton, *Loosening the Grip: A Handbook of Alcohol Information* (St. Louis: Mosby Press, 1995).

4. Michel Foucault, *Power/Knowledge: Selected Interviews and Other Writings, 1972–1977*, trans. Colin Gordon, Leo Marshall, John Mepham, and Kate Soper (New York: Pantheon Books, 1980), 176.

5. Ibid., 177.

6. Roger Penrose, *The Large, the Small, and the Human Mind* (New York: Cambridge University Press, 1999), 169-71.

7. The "mind," in this scenario, can be thought of as the interface between the brain, as a computer, and exterior experience.

8. Daniel D. Dennett, *Consciousness Explained* (Boston: Little Brown and Company, 1991), 279.

9. Kinney and Leaton, *Loosening the Grip*, 2.

10. John Scarborough, "The Opium Poppy in Hellenistic and Roman Medicine," *Drugs and Narcotics in History,* ed. Roy Porter and Mikulas Teich (New York: Cambridge University Press, 1995), 4, 5, 17.

11. Thorleif Boman, *Hebrew Thought Compared with Greek* (Philadelphia: Westminster Press, 1960), 100.

12. Emile Durkheim, *The Elementary Forms of Religious Life,* trans. Karen Fields (New York: Free Press, 1995), 438.

13. Peter L. Berger and Thomas Luckmann, *The Social Construction of Reality* (Garden City, N.Y.: Doubleday, 1966), 52, 61.

14. Karl Mannheim, *Ideology and Utopia: An Introduction to the Sociology of Knowledge,* trans. Louis Wirth and Edward Shils (San Diego: Harcourt Brace Jovanovich, 1985), 15.

15. Boman, *Hebrew Thought,* 202.

16. Terrence Deacon, *The Symbolic Species: The Co-Evolution of Language and the Brain* (New York: W. W. Norton and Co., 1997), 452.

17. Thomas Szasz, *The Manufacture of Madness: A Comparative Study of the Inquisition and the Mental Health Movement* (New York: Harper & Row, 1970), 222.

18. Ernest Becker, *The Denial of Death* (New York: Free Press, 1973), 125.

19. Ibid., 248.

20. Jenny Eliscu, "Q&A with Scott Weiland," *Rolling Stone* 874 (2 August 2001): 30.

21. Kinney and Leaton, *Loosening the Grip,* 4.

Epilogue

In place of spiritual knowledge, modern humanity is armed with technology, which includes a growing pharmacopoeia for manipulating brain processes and our experiences of the world. What we cannot overcome we can always pretend is not there. We live in an age when health, as defined by cultural institutions, replaces salvation, and medical practice is engaged in altering the consciousness of a person.[1]

In this environment, we find a growing number of people for whom drugs are a staple of life. Drugs offer a momentary experience of surpassing the dreary limits of existence, or a hope of altering a nonconforming awareness to one that fits more easily into the surrounding culture. For those purposes, drugs are not only an acceptable social practice, but also marketed as such, however illusory these goals may ultimately be.

Unfortunately for many people, some of these drugs are prohibited by a society that desires increasing control of its population. The prohibitions are especially restrictive of drugs that have intoxicant qualities, that provide brief experiences of euphoria or of a womblike security. For obvious reasons, these are also the drugs that prove most appealing in a culture whose science denies a way out of the world. As a result, many drugs users not only are routinely incarcerated, but also spend their lives feeling trapped.

Also unfortunately, there are many drug users who find they lack the ability to quit. The etiology is a mystery, but addiction becomes a life-threatening condition. The chronic use of a drug ruins bodies, destroys relationships, and places people in constant legal danger. Even worse, addiction is a condition that drug abusers have great difficulty seeing for themselves.

In that situation, the most effective remedy for addiction remains a countercultural, nonprofessional gathering of fellow addicts, who support one another, seek the help of God (as each understands God), and pursue an admittedly spiritual program. Clinical agencies, such as the agency I work for, routinely refer clients to Twelve Step meetings because the resources at our immediate disposal are inadequate, and, apart from various kinds of clinical practice, our society offers extremely little help. For people who have trouble feeling at home in such meetings, such as adolescents, the prognosis is very guarded.

This is why religious communities can offer such a needed ministry to a deserving and damaged group of people. Churches are spiritual programs, by nature, with a message and opportunity that goes beyond what a Twelve Step program is intended to offer. At the same time, in offering such ministry, the addicted can help the church regain a sense of its roots and begin to counter the dominant agenda of our culture. It is important to recognize the purposes and underlying philosophy of the drug program, and the effect that it has upon the population in obvious and subtle ways. The religious trappings of our culture are often employed in a cynical enterprise, providing spiritual cover for perspectives that deny the essence of that same religion. The result is the spiritual abandonment of people, who subsequently lack the resources to live in any meaningful manner and perish for feeling alone.

The client who most haunts me is Jessica. She was an intelligent, friendly sixteen-year-old girl who chronically smoked marijuana and had a penchant for running away from home.

As we got to know each other, I came to understand the dynamics of her home life. Her mother was an alcoholic who was rude, loud, and verbally abusive. There were times that I would call Jessica, to learn why she had missed an appointment, and hear her mother in the background, cursing at Jessica to "get the f*** off the phone." She disliked the series of men her mother engaged in relationships. She spent most of her time, when at home, sitting alone in her locked room, smoking pot and listening to music through headphones. That was her experience of peace.

It was very difficult for me, in good conscience, to tell her to stop using marijuana. She had already been in foster care, where she found more abuse. She had been in group homes. She had decided to stay with mother, come what may, and set a goal of joining the military as soon as she was eligible. It was a realistic aim, if she quit using drugs long enough to give the recruiter a clean urine test. She graduated from high school early, and as she approached the age when she could enlist, Jessica agreed to enter an inpatient rehab. We had decided that was her best chance to really become drug free.

The trouble was that social services had discontinued her Medicaid, without which she couldn't afford the treatment. I made calls, got Medicaid approval, and sent Jessica to get the paperwork. She returned on a Friday with a form that had an incorrect ID number. Because of the mistake, she could not enter the rehab clinic until Monday.

That Sunday afternoon, Jessica was found dead, her body dumped in a vacant lot. She had overdosed on heroin. Whether that was because of inexperience, or because street heroin is notoriously inconsistent in terms of strength, does not really matter. The person who abandoned her body was never found. A promising but pain-filled life was gone.

At the funeral, her mother, accompanied by her latest friend, wept. The newspaper reported that another teen druggie had died and interviewed the mother about how awful that was. I, however, knew a person, a life, a human being who had few resources, and for whom drugs appeared to offer the only relief. I knew a person who needed a place to feel welcome and a way to make sense of the life into which she had been thrown. She was a person who had been failed by her society, by her mother, and, I felt, even by me.

There are many like Jessica. I still think of her, and it gives me a sense of purpose. I can continue to reach others. And in that effort, I truly believe the church can offer a hope and a God that can be found nowhere else. It is a sacred call.

---

1. Michel Foucault, *The Birth of the Clinic: The Archaeology of Medical Perception,* trans. A. M. Sheridan Smith (New York: Pantheon Books, 1973), 198.

LINCOLN CHRISTIAN COLLEGE AND SEMINARY 114334

261. 8322
D1881

3 4711 00184 9498